THE MAFIA
IN AMERICA

THE MAFIA IN AMERICA

An Oral History

Howard Abadinsky

PRAEGER SPECIAL STUDIES • PRAEGER SCIENTIFIC

Library of Congress Cataloging in Publication Data

Abadinsky, Howard, 1941-
   The Mafia in America.

   Bibliography: p.
   1. Mafia—Case studies. 2. Organized crime—
United States. 3. Organized crime—New York
(State) 4. Organized crime—New Jersey. I. Title.
HV6446.A22   364.1′06′073   81-4338
ISBN 0-03-059587-8   AACR2

Published in 1981 by Praeger Publishers
CBS Educational and Professional Publishing
A Division of CBS, Inc.
521 Fifth Avenue, New York, New York 10175 U.S.A.

© 1981 by Praeger Publishers

123456789   145   987654321

Printed in the United States of America

To the memory of
Detective Investigator Joseph Wachtel

Preface

This is a study of Italian-American organized crime that utilizes the life history of Vito Palermo (a pseudonym) who had been involved with organized crime in the New York-New Jersey metropolitan area for more than 14 years. Vito provides data on three critical issues in organized crime.

Issue one – the structure of organized crime. Is organized crime highly complex and bureaucratic, its structure analogous to a corporate enterprise? Or is organized crime loosely structured, a network of patron-client relationships?

Issue two – membership, roles, and rules in organized crime. Is member status distinguished from associate status; if so, what are the advantages and disadvantages of membership? What are the functional roles and the operating rules in organized crime?

Issue three – the business of organized crime. What are the various sources of income for organized crime? Is it basically a provider of illegal goods and services or an extorter from those who supply them? What is the role of organized crime in conventional criminal activity such as burglary and robbery? Is organized crime a threat to legitimate business?

I was able to contact Vito through the United States Marshals Service, which administers the Witness Protection Program for the Department of Justice. Vito had been in their program as a result of his testimony against some organized crime figures in New Jersey. I met with Vito in the autumn of 1978, and he consented to a series of interviews over a period of weeks. He agreed to discuss his life, particularly his involvement in organized crime, which he refers to as the mafia. These interviews were tape-recorded, and their transcriptions provide the data for this study.

In Part I, I will trace the evolution of organized crime in the New York area to historically ground the subject. The next three chapters will provide background for each of the critical issues. In Part II the question of defining organized crime will be presented. Chapter 6 will review methodological issues in researching organized crime, and the method used in this study will be discussed. Chapter 7 presents Vito's first-person account, followed (in Chapter 8) by an analysis of the data.

Acknowledgments

I would like to thank Lynda Sharp, my editor at Praeger, for the confidence she has shown in this work. I would also like to acknowledge the assistance provided by the United States Marshals Service.

Contents

PART 1

Background

1

Evolution of Organized Crime in New York

Bell (1964) writes that "at the turn of the century the cleavage developed between the Big City and the small town conscience. Crime as a growing business was fed by the revenues from prostitution, liquor, and gambling that a wide-open urban society encouraged and that a middle-class Protestant ethos tried to suppress with a ferocity unmatched in any other civilized country" (p. 116).* Tyler (1962) notes that organized crime in America "is the product of an evolutionary process extending more than a century" (p. 89). He points out that the roots of organized crime can be found in New York decades before Prohibition. In New York the saloon-keeper, gambling house/brothel keeper, and politician were often the same person or persons. The saloon was the center of neighborhood society in lower-class environments, an important base for political activity, and in

---

*Packer (1968) contends that "regardless of what we think we are trying to do, when we make it illegal to traffic in commodities for which there is an inelastic demand, the effect is to secure a kind of monopoly profit to the entrepreneur who is willing to break the law. In effect, we say to him: 'We will set up a barrier to entry into this line of commerce by making it illegal and, therefore, risky; if you are willing to take the risk, you will be sheltered from the competition of those unwilling to do so' "(p. 279). Thus, translating morality into a statute backed by the criminal sanction does not provide for greater morality – it merely widens the scope of the law and creates both temptation and opportunity for particular social actors. As in any enterprise, the better organized are usually the more successful.

New York saloonkeepers became political powers.* They were in a position to deliver the votes of their wards, often with the help of gangs that proliferated in the ghetto areas of New York.

On September 9, 1923, the New York Times ("New Gang Methods") reminisced about the old breed of gang with its twisted sense of valor as contrasted with the current (1923) gang style with "the calculation and efficiency of an industrial tool for breaking strikes or wrecking factories" (p. 3). The Times was referring to the demise of the Shirt Tails, Dead Rabbits, Plug Uglies, Bowery Boys, Hudson Dusters, Gophers, Whyos, and the Five Points Gang. The Five Pointers were led by ex-pugilist Paul Kelly (actually Paolo Vaccarelli), and it is reputed to have had 1,500 members including Al Capone and Salvatore Lucania ("Lucky Luciano"). † Capone would eventually go to Chicago and rise to the leadership of organized crime in that city, while Luciano would do the same in New York. These gangs were used by politicians as "repeaters" (who voted early and voted often) and "sluggers," a situation that led the notorious apelike gang leader Monk Eastman (actually Edward Osterman) to utter, "Say, I cut some ice in this town. Why, I make half the big politicians" ("New Gang Methods," 1923.). Logan (1970) notes that "to keep the gang members in funds between elections, the politicians found jobs for them in the off-season months" (p. 56). They worked as lookouts, steerers, and bouncers – resident thugs for the gambling houses and brothels. Asbury (1928) notes that early in the twentieth century several gangs operating with protection from Tammany Hall (the Manhattan Democratic organization) controlled various city neighborhoods (pp. 252-53).

---

*Englemann (1979) points out that "part of the appeal of the saloon was due to the social services it provided. In saloons files of newspapers in several languages were available along with cigars, mail boxes for regular patrons, free pencils, paper, and mail services for those wishing to send letters, and information on employment. Saloons provided a warm fire in winter, public toilets, bowling alleys, billiard tables, music, singing, dancing, constant conversation, charity and charge accounts, quiet corners for students, and special rooms for weddings, union meetings, or celebrations. No other institution provided such a variety of necessary services to the public" (p. 4).

† Whenever available, I will make note of nicknames since they are quite important in organized crime. As we shall see in Chapter 7, it is not unusual for a person involved in organized crime to be known only by his nickname. Law enforcement agencies dealing with organized crime maintain extensive nickname files to enable them to identify organized crime figures.

EVOLUTION OF ORGANIZED CRIME

In Manhattan organized criminal activities were presided over by a three-man board: a representative of Tammany, the police, and Frank Farrell, the bookmaking czar who represented gambling interests. Logan (1970) points out that in the years prior to World War I, the New York City Police Department was, more or less, a branch of Tammany (p. 85). Gambling was "licensed" by Tammany leader State Senator Timothy Sullivan. When Chief of Police "Big Bill" Devery had his post abolished by the Republican-controlled legislature, Sullivan notified the city Democratic leader, "Boss" Richard Croker, that unless Devery was given an appointment to head the police, "ten thousand gamblers in the Sullivan-Devery syndicate would make no further contributions to Tammany." Devery received his appointment (Connable and Silberfarb, 1967, p. 224). When Tammany alderman Paddy Divver opposed brothels in his district, Sullivan organized a primary election against him, sending in Monk Eastman and Paul Kelly to beat and intimidate voters. Divver lost by a margin of three to one (pp. 224-39). Katcher (1959) notes that at this time the gangsters were merely errand boys for the politicians and the gamblers – they were at the bottom of the heap (pp. 74-75). This would change with the advent of Prohibition.

ARNOLD ROTHSTEIN

Timothy Sullivan eventually became insane, was committed, escaped, and died on some railroad tracks in Westchester. Charles Murphy, like Sullivan, a former saloonkeeper, became Tammany leader. Murphy changed operations; open gambling and prostitution were ended, and total immunity for gangsters was withdrawn. He also moved to cut down the power of the police who, on occasion, had challenged the politicians (Katcher, 1959, pp. 95-96). Murphy concluded "that the use of the police as major graft collectors was an antiquated concept" (p. 96). Modern organization was needed – a conduit between the politicians and the gamblers who would be organized into a dues-paying trade association as were the brothel owners. Arnold Rothstein was selected as the conduit (Logan, 1970, p. 340).

"A. R." or "The Brain," as Damon Runyon called him, was born in New York in 1882 and served as the inspiration for Meyer Wolfsheim in The Great Gatsby (1925) and for Nathan Detroit in the musical Guys and Dolls. His father was an Orthodox Jew who became a successful and widely respected businessman. Arnold was also successful and respected, but his business included gambling, bootlegging, diamond and drug smuggling, and labor racketeering. He is viewed as the catalyst for the organized crime that eventually developed out of Prohibition in New York.

PROHIBITION

Fried (1980) suggests that after World War I the age of the Jewish gangster was coming to a close. Jewish immigration had virtually ceased; economic conditions had improved; the attractions of unionism, socialism, and Zionism, along with the growth of communal groups, had strengthened the Jewish community. Then came Prohibition — January 16, 1920, the day the Volstead Act became effective: "Prohibition could be likened to a deus ex machina: an unseen, unanticipated force that suddenly reverses the action and brings something calamitously new in its train" (p. 93). Logan (1970) points out that Prohibition turned gangs into empires (p. 341). The New York Times ("Schultz," 1933) points to the transition made by Arthur Flegenheimer, "Dutch Schultz." In 1919 he was sentenced to imprisonment for unlawful entry; by 1933 he was "a wealthy man with widespread interests," the "beer baron of the Bronx" (p. 23). When Prohibition began Schultz was working for a trucking concern whose owner quickly switched to the beer business. By 1928 Schultz was the owner of a speakeasy and a fleet of trucks and became a major beer distributor. With a vicious crew of gunmen he expanded into the territory of rival beer producers. The Jewish Prohibition gangster, Fried (1980) points out, was a tough among toughs. The Jewish community provided very little support for the alcohol business — they were negligible consumers. To capture lucrative markets, Jewish gangsters had to compete in gentile neighborhoods (pp. 102-3).

Other Jewish gangsters were active in New York. The "Bug and Meyer Gang" was headed by Benjamin ("Bugsy") Siegel and Meyer Lansky. They rented out high-speed cars and trucks to haul bootleg whiskey and provided the gunmen to protect the shipments from hijackers (Messick, 1973, p. 21). Louis ("Lepke") Buchalter and Jacob ("Gurrah") Shapiro revolutionized labor and industrial racketeering: "Instead of using his sluggers and gunmen to terrorize labor unions during strike periods, Lepke worked them directly into the unions. By threat and by violence they controlled one local after another" (Berger, 1944, p. 30). Manufacturers who hired Lepke to deal with the unions "soon found themselves wriggling helplessly in the grip of Lepke's smooth but deadly organization. He moved in on them as he had on the unions" (p. 30). Buchalter and Shapiro were invited into the fur industry where the Protective Fur Dressers Corporation was attempting to put an end to cutthroat competition. They were notified when fur dealers, dressers, or manufacturers were "not cooperating." Bombings, assaults, acid, and arson were the responses (Block, 1975, pp. 93-97).*

---

*Seidman (1938) contends that as Prohibition was drawing to a close, and with the onset of the Great Depression, the leaders of organized crime began searching for other areas of profit. The result was a significant increase in labor and industrial racketeering.

During Prohibition two political/criminal factions emerged in New York. One was headed by James J. Hines, a Tammany renegade with ties to Dutch Schultz, Ownie ("The Killer") Madden, Bill Dwyer, Vannie Higgens, and Larry Fay. The other was headed by Albert C. Marrinelli, a port warden and Tammany stalwart, who had ties to Italian gangsters Joe Masseria, Lucky Luciano, Frankie (Yale) Uale, Francesco Castiglia ("Frank Costello"), and Albert Anastasia (Katcher, 1959, pp. 260-64). Rothstein had important ties to both factions.* Fried (1980) points out that the violence that was spawned by competitive efforts during Prohibition eventually led to a level of rationalization that had not heretofore been achieved by gangsters. Ethnic rivalries became secondary as gang leaders, mostly Italian and Jewish, formed alliances (p. 122).

CASTELLAMMARESE WAR

Events in Italy impacted on American organized crime. Cesare Mori, acting with unlimited police powers conferred by Benito Mussolini, moved against mafiosi in Sicily. As a result many fled to the United States, and a few became important organized crime figures — men such as Joseph Bonanno, Joseph Profaci, and Salvatore Maranzano. By 1930 there were two major factions in Italian-American organized crime: one headed by Maranzano and the other by Joe ("The Boss") Masseria. The struggle that eventually ensued between these two groups came to be known as the Castellammarese War, since many of the Maranzano group came from the small town of Castellammare del Golfo in Sicily. Masseria was a Neapolitan and his group included other non-Sicilians who were to play important roles in American organized crime: Vito Genovese, John Doto ("Joe Adonis"), and Frank Costello. They were allied with such non-Italians as Lansky and Siegel. The Maranzano group consisted mainly of Sicilians, especially the "moustaches," tradition-oriented immigrants who often sported large moustaches. As the war turned against Masseria, five of his leading men, including Luciano and Genovese, went over to Maranzano. On April 15, 1931, they were waiting to have dinner with Masseria. "Masseria drove his steel-armored sedan, a massive car with plate glass an inch thick in all its windows, to a garage near the Nuovo Villa Tammaro at 2,715 West Fifteenth Street, Coney Island, and parked it. Then he went into the restaurant." After dinner he was shot to death ("Racket Chief Slain," 1931, p. 1).

---

*Arnold Rothstein was murdered in 1928, and although the murder has never been solved, it appeared to have been the result of a personal dispute over a card game and gambling debt. Rothstein left an estate that was appraised at $1,757,572. His hidden assets, of course, are not known (S. Smith, 1963, p. 96).

Talese reports (1971, p. 191):

> After Masseria's funeral, Maranzano presided at a meeting attended by 500 people in a hired hall in the Bronx and explained that the days of shooting were over and that a period of harmony was about to begin. He then presented them with his plan of organization, one loosely based on Caesar's military command – the individual gangs each would be commanded by a capo, or boss, under whom would a sottocapo. underboss, and beneath the underboss would be caporegimi, lieutenants who would supervise the squads of soldiers. Each unit would be known as a family and would operate within prescribed territorial areas. Over all the family bosses would be a capo di tutti capi, a boss of all bosses, and it was this title that Maranzano bequeathed to himself.

This is essentially the version provided by Valachi, who claims to have been present at the meeting (Maas, 1968, pp. 106-7).

On September 10, 1931, four men carrying pistols entered a suite at 230 Park Avenue. "One of them ordered the seven men and Miss Francis Samuels, a secretary, to line up against the wall. The others stalked into the private office of Salvatore Maranzano. There was a sound of voices raised in angry dispute; blows, struggling, and finally pistol shots, and the four men dashed out of the suite." Maranzano was found with "his body riddled with bullets and punctured with knife wounds" ("Gang Kills Suspect," 1931, p. 1). The killers are believed to have been Jews (who Maranzano would not recognize) sent by Lansky at the behest of Luciano. They flashed badges and Maranzano apparently thought them to be federal agents who had visited his office before. The killers, using knives, attempted to kill Maranzano silently. When he fought back, they shot him. The episode is considered highly significant, because it marked the ascent of Luciano and the "Americanized" Italian gangsters at the expense of the mustaches. The men around Luciano at this time became important organized crime figures, their power extending into the 1960s and 1970s.

ITALIAN DOMINATION OF ORGANIZED CRIME

Dutch Schultz recognized that Prohibition was going to come to an end, and the beer baron expanded his activities accordingly. In the Bronx and Upper Manhattan he took over the numbers lottery from black and Hispanic operators (Sann, 1971, pp. 150-63) and also moved into labor racketeering. ("Gang Linked to Union," 1934, p. 8). However, Schultz experienced difficulties with the Internal Revenue Service and went into hiding for 18 months. He surrendered to federal authorities at the end of 1934, and his first trial ended in a hung jury; his second, in an acquittal. During his legal difficulties, Luciano and other gangsters began moving in on Schultz's operations. In 1935 Schultz was murdered in a Newark tavern on the order of Luciano and other prominent Italian and non-Italian gang chieftains.

With Schultz's death, his organization disintegrated. The organizations of other non-Italian organized crime figures similarly withered with the leader's demise, imprisonment, or retirement. While there were Irish organized crime figures in New York and some important Jewish old-timers (e.g., Lansky and Abner ("Longie")Zwillman of New Jersey), in urban areas that had a sizable Italian population such as New York, they were the dominant group in organized crime. In a pattern that Ianni (1974) refers to as "ethnic succession," the Irish and Jews used the "Queer Ladder" of organized crime into respectable society (Bell, 1964) – their progeny no longer looked to organized crime for advancement. The Italians, on the other hand, still had available a continuous supply of young aspirants from which to recruit.

Toby (1958) notes that while the Jews and Italians came to the United States in large numbers at about the same time (the Irish came considerably earlier), their attitudes toward education differed significantly. In the United States, intellectual achievement was valued by the Jews: "Second-generation Jewish students did homework diligently, got high grades, went to college in disproportionate numbers, and scored high on intelligence tests" (p. 548). Immigrants from southern Italy, however,

> tended to regard formal education as either a frill or as a source of dangerous ideas from which the minds of the young should be protected. They remembered Sicily, where a child who attended school regularly was a rarity. There, youngsters were needed not(sic) only to help on the farm. Equally important was the fact that hardworking peasants could not understand why their children should learn classical Italian (which they would not speak at home) or geography (when they would not travel in their lifetime more than a few miles from their birthplace). Sicilian parents suspected that education was an attempt on the part of Roman officials to subvert the authority of the family. In the United States, many South Italian immigrants maintained the same attitudes. They resented compulsory school attendance laws and prodded their children to go to work and become economic assets as soon as possible. They encouraged neglect of school-work and even truancy. They did not realize that education has more importance in an urban-industrial society than in a semi-feudal one. With supportive motivation from home lacking, the second-generation Italian boys did not make the effort of Jewish contemporaries. Their teachers tried to stuff the curriculum into their heads in vain. Their lack of interest was reflected not only in low marks, retardation, truancy, and early school leavings; it even resulted in poor scores on intelligence tests. They accepted their

parents' conception of the school as worthless and thereby lost their best opportunity for social ascent. (P. 548)

Some of these youngsters who did not reconcile themselves to remaining at the bottom moved into organized crime.

In the New York City area, five major organized crime "families" emerged, and their lineage can be traced back to the 1930s and the Castellammarese War:

Lucky Luciano (whose family leadership went to Vito Genovese, then to Frank Costello, and back to Genovese),

Vincent Mangano (whose disappearance in 1951 remains unsolved and made way for the leadership to pass to Albert Anastasia; when Anastasia was murdered in 1957, leadership went to Carlo Gambino),

Gaetana Gagliano (who died of natural causes in 1953, with family leadership going to Thomas Lucchese),

Joseph Bonanno (whose leadership ended in 1964 during the Banana War),* and

Joseph Profaci (whose family leadership was unsuccessfully challenged by the Gallo brothers;†when he died of cancer in 1962, he was succeeded by Joseph Colombo).

Except for Bonanno, as of this writing, all of these persons are deceased. However, family continuity is reputedly still intact. Of these five major families, three will play some part in this study: the Mangano family, headed by Carlo Gambino; the Luciano family, headed by Vito Genovese; and the Bonanno family.

_____

*See Talese (1971) for a journalist's participant observation view of the Banana War.

†See Martin (1963) for a ranking police officer's firsthand look at the Gallo brothers "insurrection." For a first-person account of these events by Joey Gallo's bodyguard, see Diapoulos and Linakis (1976).

2

The Structure of Organized Crime

To understand Italian organized crime, Cressey (1969) suggests we look at the Sicilian mafia:* "While we are confident that American organized crime is not merely the Sicilian Mafia transplanted, the similarities between the two organizations are direct and too great to be ignored" (p. 8). He argues that there is a remarkable similarity between the structure and cultural values of both the Sicilian mafia and Italian-American organized crime (p. 25). Using a bureaucratic analogy, Cressey (1967a) refers to a crime "family" unit as a monopolistic corporation (p. 31). The Task Force on Organized Crime (1967) outlines the structure:

> Each family is headed by one man, the "boss," whose primary functions are maintaining order and maximizing profits. Subject only to the possibility of being overruled by the national advisory group, which will be discussed below, his authority in all matters relating to his family is absolute.
>
> Beneath each boss is an "underboss," the vice-president or deputy director of the family. He collects information for the boss; he relays messages to him and passes his instructions down to his own underlings. In the absence of the boss, the underboss acts for him.
>
> On the same level as the underboss, but operating in a staff capacity, is the consigliere, who is a counselor, or advisor. Often an elder member of the family who has partially retired from a career in crime, he gives advice to family members, including the boss and underboss, and thereby enjoys considerable influence and power.

---

*For reasons that will be explained shortly, I will always use the form mafia, although quotes from other writers will appear in their original form.

11

Below the level of the underboss are the caporegime, some of whom serve as buffers between the top members of the family and the lower-echelon personnel. To maintain their insulation from the police, the leaders of the hierarchy (particularly the boss) avoid direct communication with the workers. All commands, information, complaints, and money flow back and forth through a trusted go-between. A caporegima fulfilling this buffer capacity, however, unlike the underboss, does not make decisions or assume any of the authority of his boss.

Other caporegime serve as chiefs of operating units. The number of men supervised in each unit varies with the size and activities of particular families. Often the caporegima has one or two associates who work closely with him, carrying orders, information, and money to the men who belong to his unit. From a business standpoint, the caporegima is analogous to plant supervisor or sales manager.

The lowest level "members" of a family are the soldati, the soldiers or "button" men who report to the caporegime. A soldier may operate a particular illicit enterprise, e.g., a loan-sharking operation, a dice game, a lottery, a bookmaking operation, a smuggling operation, on a commission basis, or he may "own" the enterprise and pay a portion of its profit to the organization, in return for the right to operate. Partnerships are common between two or more soldiers and between soldiers and men higher up in the hierarchy. Some soldiers and most upper-echelon members have interests in more than one business.

Beneath the soldiers in the hierarchy are large numbers of employees and commission agents who are not members of the family and are not necessarily of Italian descent. These are the people who do most of the actual work in the various enterprises. They have no buffers or other insulation from law enforcement. They take bets, drive trucks, answer telephones, sell narcotics, tend to the stills, work in the legitimate businesses.* (Pp. 7-8)

Cressey (1969) states that "the authority structure we have outlined for Costa Nostra resembles the structure of the Sicilian-Italian Mafia" (p. 141). However, bureaucratic structure is actually a characteristic of the

---

*According to Cressey (1969) there are at least 24 of these tightly knit crime family units that comprise a nationwide confederation ruled by a commission made up of the leaders of the most powerful of the families (pp. x-xi). For an opposing view, see Morris and Hawkins (1970).

Cosa Nostra is the name by which Cressey refers to Italian organized crime in the United States.

Camorra of Naples, an organization about which Cressey makes no mention in his works, and not of the mafia of Sicily.*

THE MAFIA AND THE CAMORRA

About 90 percent of the Italians who came to the United States from 1875 until 1920 came from the south, the mezzogiorno (Gambino, 1974, p. 3). The history of southern Italy is the history of repression — political, social, and economic — a succession of foreign rulers culminating in a revolution in 1860 that eventually united Italy. For most of the people in the south, however, little changed. Instead of foreign repression, the contadini ("peasants") of the south were repressed by Italians from the north.

This southern experience dates back 700 years, and it led to the development of a culture that stressed the variables necessary for survival in a hostile environment. The only basis for loyalty was the family, sangu de me sangu ("blood of my blood"). Gambino describes the family of southern Italy:

> The famiglia was composed of all of one's blood relatives, including those relatives Americans would consider very distant cousins, aunts and uncles, an extended clan whose genealogy was traced through paternity. The clan was supplemented through an important custom known as comparatico or comparaggio (godparenthood), through which carefully selected outsiders became to an important (but incomplete) extent members of the family. (P. 3)

Gambino notes that the family patriarch (capo di famiglia) arbitrated all ambiguous situations, and the family was organized hierarchically: "One had absolute responsibilities to family superiors and absolute rights to be demanded from subordinates in the hierarchy" (p. 4). Barzini (1977) describes the dynamic qualities of the southern Italian famiglia:

> The family, first source of power, had to be made prosperous, respected, and feared with antlike tenacity; it was enlarged (like dynasties of old) by suitable marriages, strengthened by alliances with families of equal status, by negotiated submission to more powerful ones, or by establishing its domination over weaker ones. (P. 36)

---

*Bureaucracies are organized hierarchically with a strict chain of command from top to bottom. They create an elaborate division of labor, and detailed general rules and regulations govern all conduct in the pursuit of official duties. Personnel are selected primarily on the basis of competence and specialized skill (Wrong, 1970, p. 32).

The southern Italian developed an ideal of manliness, omertà (from uomo, "man," and refers to "behaving like a man"), which included non-cooperation with authorities, self-control in the face of adversity, and the vendetta in which any offense or slight to family must be avenged, no matter what the consequences or how long it takes. Out of this history and culture developed the mafia and the Camorra.

MAFIA

Chandler (1975) traces the origins of the mafia to fifteenth century Spain and a secret criminal society called the Garduña (p. 6). Spanish kings ruled Naples during most of the years between 1504 and 1860, and Chandler argues that the Garduña* reached Naples in the sixteenth century where it took the form of the Camorra (pp. 14-15). The Italian revolutionary Giuseppe Mazzini had a close relationship with the Camorra, and Chandler states that Mazzini brought it to Sicily in the form of a secret revolutionary society (pp. 26-27). The name, Chandler argues, by which it became known was derived from the initials of Mazzini Autorizzi Furti, Incedi, Avvelenamenti (MAFIA) – "Mazzini Authorizes Theft, Arson, Poisoning," the slogan of his revolutionary organization. Inciardi (1975) disputes this account.

A scholarly analysis of the Italian language during these periods, combined with an examination of Sicilian history, suggests that such derivations represent little more than pure fiction. More laudable explanations of Mafia come from Sicilian historical and literary works that link its root and meaning to elements prevailing within Sicilian culture. Mafia is seemingly Sicilian-Arabic, descending from the etuma hafa: to preserve, protect, and act as guardian; from mo' hafi: friend or companion; from mo' hafah: to defend; and from mo' hafiat: preservation, safety, power, integrity, strength, and a state that designates the remedy of damage and ill. That the Arabic mo' hafiat became mafiat by ellision, and mafia by apocope, can be drawn from (Giuseppe) Pitre who described mafia as a dialect term common in pre-1860 Palermo. It expressed "beauty and excellence," united with notions of "superiority" and "bravery"; in reference to man, it also meant: "the consciousness of being a man," "assurance of the mind," "boldness" but never "defiance," and "arrogance" but never

---

*Simmel (1950) refers to the Garduñas as a secret criminal society with ties to the Inquisition operating in Spain from the seventeenth to the beginning of the nineteenth century (p. 371). In Spanish a garduna is a marten and the term is used to refer to a "sneak thief."

"haughtiness." Thus, both Arabic-Sicilian references and common Palermitani usage contributed to Mafia's meanings: protection against the arrogance of the powerful, remedy to any damage, sturdiness of body, strength and serenity of spirit, and the best and most exquisite part of life. (Pp. 112-13, references deleted)

Barzini (1965) separates mafia, referring to a state of mind and a philosophy of life, from Mafia, the illegal secret organization. The former he notes is shared by all Sicilians, the honest and the criminal, as "they must aid each other, side with their friends and fight the common enemies even when the friends are wrong and the enemies are right; each must defend his dignity at all costs and never allow the smallest slight to go unavenged; they must keep secrets and always be aware of official authorities and laws" (pp. 253-54). Barzini points out that the two (mafia and Mafia) are closely related – that Mafia could not flourish without mafia (p. 256).

Pantaleone (1966) states that mafia evolved out of the companies of private guards (compagnie d'armi) on the manorial estates in Sicily. Out of these eventually developed the gabelloti, mafiosi who ruled, and eventually came to own, the estates. The mafia controlled the families living on the land – and thus their votes and the politics of the area. Political control enabled the mafia to gain immunity for criminal activities (pp. 32-33). According to Pantaleone, the mafia eventually moved from its rural base into urban areas; and "by the beginning of this century the Mafia was very (sic) flourishing in all the urban centres, particularly in western Sicily" (p. 34). Actually, the mafia never developed in the eastern end of the island. Hess (1973) argues that the urban mafia has more in common with American urban gangsters, whose pattern the new mafiosi copied, than with the mafia of rural Sicily (pp. 162-63). The men hired by the landlords, gabelloti, and the men they hired, campieri, earned rispetto ("respect") because of their capacity for violence and their ability to provide access to resources, particularly land, for their followers (Blok, 1974 p. 62). On one level of society they kept the peasants in line, while at a higher level they lent political support to any government that provided them with enough freedom to continue operating in western Sicily (pp. 75-76). The Bourbon government depended on private groups to maintain law and order in the rugged terrain of Sicily. These private groups, compagnie d'armi, mixed with bandits and the gabelloti: "To a large extent what was later called mafia coincided with these associations of armed strong men and their followers who exercised jurisdiction on the local level in conjunction with formal authority" (p. 94).

Blok notes that the mafia (he always uses the lower case and italics) is not a secret society but an entity that developed from an association between violent peasant entrepreneurs who were charged with maintaining order and security on the large estates of absentee landlords and bandits. These entrepreneurs came to represent a class of intermediaries between the aristocracy and the peasants – "individuals who operate in different social realms and who succeed in maintaining a grip on the intrinsic tensions by means of physical force" (p. xxviii). As intermediaries the mafiosi exploit communication gaps between the peasant and the wider society, and they maintain their position as intermediaries through the systematic application of political power and physical force (p. 8).

Blok notes that although they date back to the early nineteenth century, the term mafia was not used until 1868 (p. 95). Gambino (1974) suggests that the term mafia or mafiosi was seldom used in Sicily; instead members of the "society" were gli uomini qualificati ("qualified men") or gli amici degli amici ("friends of friends") (p. 296). He reports that the mafia leaders, padrini ("godfathers"), formed a confederation by the late nineteenth century and a capo di tutti capi ("boss of bosses") emerged (p. 297). This is scoffed at by Hess (1973) who argues, "Mafia is neither an organisation nor a secret society, but a method" (p. 127). A "method" does not have a "boss or bosses." In Sicily, "a mafiosi is simply a courageous fellow who won't stand any nonsense from anyone" (p. 1). These mafiosi, "men in whom the mafioso attitude is particularly strong come together in a kind of instinctive solidarity in order to support one another mutually in the pursuit of their aims" (p. 10). They form "small clique-like associations which are independent of each other but maintain relations with one another" (p. 11). The mafioso succeeds because he commands a partito – a network of relationships whereby he is able to act as an intermediary providing services that include votes and violence for the holders of institutionalized power (p. 12). Thus, he gains immunity to carry out his activities.

Each village in western Sicily has its own cosca ("clique") – larger ones have two – and collectively these cosche are referred to as the mafia, although there has never been one mafia. While mafiosi maintain relationships with amici from other villages, in opposition to Gambino's assertion, Blok (1974) states that there has never been one hierarchical organization of mafiosi throughout Sicily (p. 145). One becomes a member of a cosca gradually and "not through any kind of formal initiation." Hess (1973) points out that "the cosca is not a group to which initiation would be possible," being too informal a structure (p. 80). He concludes that "the cosca is not a group with a rigid organisation, let alone a società – 'friends of friends,' that is an exact description of the fluctuating, oscillating bonds along the relationship lines described" (p. 88).

CAMORRA

In contrast to the mafia, the Camorra was a secret criminal society that Hobsbawn (1959) notes was "rather tightly, centrally and hierarchically organized" (p. 55). It even had a "boss of bosses" (capo in testa).* The

---

*For a detailed description of the structure of the Camorra, see Serao (1911a, 1911b).

Camorra developed in the Spanish prisons during the Bourbon rule of the Two Sicilies, early in the nineteenth century. The members of this society eventually moved their control of the prisons into Naples proper, McConaughy (1931) reports:

> The Camorra in Naples was organized as openly and carefully as a public school system, or an efficient political machine in one of our own cities. Naples was divided into twelve districts, and each of these into a number of sub-districts. Although burglary and other remunerative felonies were not neglected, extortion was the principal industry; and the assassination of an inconvenient person could be purchased by any one with the price. In the case of a friend in need, a murder could be arranged without any cost — a simple gesture of affection. (P. 244)

An English diplomat (quoted in Hibbert, 1966) in Naples during the 1860s observed:

> There was no class, high or low, that had not its representatives among the members of the Society which was a vast organised association for the extortion of blackmail in every conceivable shape and form. Officials, officers of the King's Household, the police and others were affiliated with the most desperate of the criminal classes in carrying out the depredations, and none was too high or too low to escape them. If a petition was to be presented to the Sovereign or to a Minister it had to be paid for; at every gate of the town, Camorristi were stationed to exact a toll of each cart or donkey load brought to market by the peasants; and on getting in a hackney carrosel in the street, I have seen one of the band run up and get his fee from the driver. No one thought of refusing to pay, for the consequences of a refusal were too well known, anyone rash enough to demur being apt to be found soon after mysteriously stabbed by some unknown individual, whom the police were careful never to discover.

Ianni (1972) writes that after 1830 "they were more efficiently organized than the police, and set up a parallel system of law in the typical southern Italian style" (p. 22). When Giuseppe Garibaldi became active in the Two Sicilies, the Bourbon king actually turned police powers over to the Camorra, and those in jail were set free. The Camorra constituted not only the de facto but also the legally constituted police power in Naples (McConaughy, 1931, p. 245). Gambino (1974) suggests that the Camorra was at the peak of its power from 1880 until 1900 (p. 292). "If they so decided, there would not be, in some regions, a single vote cast for a candidate for the Chamber of Deputies who was opposed to their man" (p. 246).

ORGANIZED CRIME AS A PATRIMONIAL ORGANIZATION

The cultural heritage of the southern Italian (which includes the city of Naples and the province of Calabria* as well as Sicily) provided a natural pattern of organization, patrimonial, as opposed to bureaucratic (Collins, 1975):

> Patrimonial organization, most characteristic of traditional societies, centers around families, patrons and their clients, and other personalistic networks. The emphasis is on traditional rituals that demonstrate the emotional bonds among men; the world is divided into those whom one can trust because of strongly legitimated personal connections, and the rest of the world from whom nothing is to be expected that cannot be exacted by cold-blooded bargaining or force. In modern bureaucratic organization, by contrast, personal ties are weaker, less ritualized, and emotionally demonstrative; in their place is the allegiance to a set of abstract rules and positions. (P. 65, n.)

Ianni (1972) argues that Italian-American crime syndicates can be explained by an examination of kinship networks (the subtitle of his book is (Kinship and Social Control in Organized Crime). This contention is supported by family ties between leading Italian-American organized crime figures. For example, Salvatore ("Bill") Bonanno, son of Joseph Bonanno, is married to Rosalie Profaci, the niece of Joseph Profaci; the daughter of Carlo Gambino is married to the son of Thomas Lucchese; Stefano Magadinno, Buffalo crime family boss, is Joseph Bonanno's cousin; two of Joseph Profaci's daughters married into the Joseph Zerrilli and William Toco crime families of Detroit.

Barzini (1965) states that "in order to beat rival organizations, criminals of Sicilian descent reproduced the kind of illegal groups they had belonged to in the old country and employed the same rules to make them invincible" (p. 273). Gambino (1974) adds that although southern Italian characteristics do not dispose men toward crime, "where the mode of life has been impressed onto organized crime it has made it difficult to combat effectively the criminal activity" (p. 304). Hence, the irony: southern Italian peasant characteristics mitigate against socioeconomic success in urban

---

*Calabria is the home of the Onerate Società ("Honored Society"), often referred to as the Brotherhood. This secret organization mixed political insurrection with banditry and had many of the characteristics of the mafia.

America and impel some toward organized crime, which these same characteristics tend to make successful.*

PATRON-CLIENT RELATIONSHIPS

Boissevain (1974) describes a social network:

The social relations in which every individual is embedded may be viewed as a network. This social network may, at one level of abstraction, be looked upon as a scattering of points connected by lines. The points, of course, are persons, and the lines are social relations. Each person can thus be viewed as a star from which lines radiate to points, some of which are connected to each other. These form his first order or primary network zone. But those persons are also in contact with others whom our central person does not know, but with whom he could come into contact via members of his first order zone. These are often important friends-of-friends. They form what might be called his second order zone. This process can be carried out at still further removes so that we can theoretically speak not only of a person's second, but also of his third, fourth and Nth order zones. In fact, all of society can be viewed as a network, and via links in his various zones, an individual can eventually get in touch with every other person. When I use the term network here, however, I use it chiefly in an egocentric sense, as the chains of persons with whom a given person is in actual contact, and their interconnection. (P. 24)

Boissevain states that while every individual provides a point at which networks interact, "not everyone displays the same interest in and talent for cultivating relationships with strategic persons and manipulating these for profits" (p. 146). The patron is such a person. (Boissevain distinguishes between a patron and a broker, but I will include both functions under the term patron since "they are often found in combination" (P. 147).)

---

*A study by Cornelisen (1980) of southern Italian immigrants in West Germany reveals an interesting contract with this American experience. Cornelisen notes the southerner's distrust of government: "They must outwit it, twist its laws, circumvent them in some way to live, not to be the victims of government" (p. 165). However, she points out, when confronted with a government (West Germany) that administers law in accord with principles of justice, equality before the law, and so on, the southern Italian immigrant responds with respect and obedience. If Cornelisen is correct, Italian-American organized crime can also be explained in terms of the administration of justice in the United States.

The patron places people in touch with one another directly or indirectly for profit; he is a professional manipulator of people and information who brings about communication for profit (p. 148). Hess (1973) refers to this arrangement as partito whereby most clients have no relations between each other except through the patron (p. 82). Boissevain (1974) points out that a successful patron requires a great deal of free time.

> A person who has more time to devote to the management of his social relations is more likely to have more multiplex social relations and to be better informed than others. These are assets for a broker. To make a profit from his social relations, he has to be able to devote time to servicing them. This is essential for the success of his enterprise. A person whose occupation allows him to invest time in servicing relations (can be an effective patron). (P. 157)

Because they need not work regular hours, organized crime figures, especially those in middle- and upper-echelon positions, are able to be effective patrons.

Wolf (1966) points out that when a social exchange becomes unbalanced, we have a patron-client relationship: the patron protects his client against both the legal and illegal exactions of authority. The client pays back, often in intangible assets, for example, esteem and loyalty, thus making the relationship reciprocal (pp. 16-17). As will be seen in Chapter 7, in organized crime the client pays back with rispetto. Wolf notes that the patron may also act as a power broker between the client and the wider society, both legitimate and illegitimate (p. 18). He points out that the patron-client relationship can be seen in the kinship pattern discussed in Ianni's (1972) work.

SUMMARY OF ISSUE ONE

Is Italian organized crime complex, best characterized by corporate analogies as a bureaucratic entity, or does it operate as a network of kinship and patron-client relationships? Does its structure come closer to the Camorra or the mafia?

3
Membership, Roles, and Rules in Organized Crime

Cressey (1969) contends that after the Castellammarese War Luciano became something of an unofficial "boss of bosses" in the New York area, and he ordered "membership books" closed (p. 45). The reason was reportedly to maintain the status quo between the relative strengths of the families (pp. 45, 157-58). To open the books, agreement must be reached among the families (p. 46). According to Cressey, the books have been opened intermittently over the years since 1931, but the concept of membership remains intact (p. 45).

The incarceration or death of a member, Cressey notes, does little to affect the family's activities: "For each vacant Cosa Nostra membership position there are at least a hundred applicants" (p. 291). However, he provides very little in the way of an explanation of the benefits of membership as opposed to some type of associate status. There is, Cressey notes, some sense of belonging, that one is a "stand-up guy" occupying a position of honor and respect (p. 236). This hardly distinguishes organized crime from the Boy Scouts or the Fraternal Order of Police.

A. Anderson (1979) reports that the family she studied had four types of associates:

Category A (close) Associates. The category A associate fulfills the basic requirement for membership in the group in that he is of Italian national origin. He may aspire to membership, or he may have been considered for membership in the past and been rejected. He is actively engaged in the activities of the group, either in illegal markets or legitimate business, and associates closely with two or more members. If he is engaged in legal activities, he has firsthand knowledge of the group's illegal activities. In short, he is an associate of the group rather than of an individual member and probably gets many, but not all, benefits of membership.

Category B Associates. The category B associate may or may not fulfill membership eligibility requirements. He works for one member of the group as an employee, usually in illegal activities such as gambling or loansharking. Insofar as he is protected from the activities of law enforcement officials, he is protected by the individual who employs him and not by the group.

Category C Associates. The category C associate may, in rare cases, fulfill membership eligibility requirements, but he probably does not. He manages, as a professional, a legitimate business financed by members of the organized crime group. Although he may be a dishonest businessman and may at times be required by the group to operate the business in an illegal or unethical manner, or may do so on his own, he is basically a businessman rather than a gangster. The owners of the business, of which he may be one, depend on his professional skills to make the business successful.

Category D Associates. The category D associate is the professional lawyer, accountant, or bail bondsman whose main clients are the members of the organized crime group, and the businessman who deals with members of organized criminal groups. Also included in this category are co-investors in legitimate business who function as equals with the investing members of the group. They may manage the business in which they are co-investors, but as equals rather than employees. (Pp. 39-40)

Unfortunately, Anderson does not indicate why an otherwise eligible person would be rejected for membership. She also fails to provide us with the benefits of membership as opposed to those that accompany associate status.

Various portions of the "De Cavalcante Tapes* refer to membership. De Cavalcante (D), Ray ("Gyp") De Carlo (DC), and Anthony ("Tony Boy") Boiardo (B) are the participants in the following excerpt:

---

*On June 10, 1969, documents based on electronic surveillance by the Federal Bureau of Investigation (FBI) were made public as part of a court case. One of the documents covers the period from May 7, 1964, to July 12, 1965, with some material from 1962, and became known as the "De Cavalcante Tapes" because the central figure is Sam ("The Plumber") de Cavalcante. He was the boss of a small New Jersey family and the conversations took place in de Cavalcante's plumbing firm's office. The documents consist of verbatim transcripts and log summaries of what was intercepted.

B: My father said you must be made twenty-five to thirty years ago.
D: No. Twenty years. About the same as you Ray.
DC: Around 1945.
D: No, you wasn't – '45?
DC: Wait a minute, my father died in '44. . . .
D: When we had the game in Princeton you were already made.
DC: Well – '47.
D: I was supposed to be made in Philadelphia.
B: You were made with the "Blade," weren't you?
D: No, he was made before the "Blade." Two or three years before the "Blade."
DC: Me and Si were made at the same time in Carmine Battaglia's house.*

Other portions of the tapes indicate that membership is controlled by the "commission." At one point Albert Anastasia was criticized (and may have been executed) for making too many members, apparently without authorization. There was fear expressed that he may have allowed FBI agents into the organization. Another portion refers to some benefits of membership and deals with de Cavalcante's efforts at securing union jobs for members of the Gambino family, apparently to build a good relationship with the most powerful of the bosses on the commission. De Cavalcante is upset that his friends from the Gambino family have to suffer the indignity of going to the union hiring hall for work. De Cavalcante (D) is talking to Joe Sferra (S), a member of de Cavalcante's family and a union business agent.

D: Joe, over here, even if he's not with us, he's still a friend of ours.
S: This guy is only home one day. He got laid off Thursday.
D: I know . . . .He told me he was laid off. I told him. . . .
S: So what's he run to you for? Don't I know it? He's got a lot of nerve.
D: Nerve or no nerve, you know I promised Carl Gambino that we'd treat their men better than own people. And I want it to be that way.
S: Sam, there are amici nostri ("friends of ours") that belong with us that got laid off the same job, too.
D: I know that. But I want these people – I don't want that as long as they're amici nostri that they have to go to the hall. . . .You see,

---

*Being "made" a member of a family may actually be akin to the Italian custom of comparatico ("ritual kindship").

Joe, over here I'm trying to build a good relationship with everybody on the commission. Our brigata is small, but we could do things as good as anybody else. And I told you, as long as they are amici nostri, I don't want them to go to the hall. I want them to keep working before anybody else.

It is of additional interest to note that de Cavalcante is talking about legitimate construction jobs, hard labor. Obviously, organized crime is not always lucrative for all of its members, another reason to restrict membership. One excerpt deals with this issue and mentions an apparent commission ban on involvement in narcotics. De Cavalcante (D) is talking Anthony ("Little Pussy") Russo (R), an underboss in his family.

R: Do you know how many of our friends are on heists?
D: They can't support themselves.
R: Do you know how many guys in Chicago are peeling(safecracking)? Do you know how many friends of ours in New York that made it, peeling. What they gonna do? Half these guys are handling junk. Now there's a law out that they can't touch it. They have no other way of making a living so what can they do? All right, we're fortunate enough that we moved around and didn't have to resort to that stuff. We had legitimate things going as well as horses, numbers, and everything. What are the other poor suckers going to do? (He then goes on to complain about having to help out "deadheads" from the New York families.)

In the May 23, 1979, indictment, State of New Jersey v. Ruggerio Boiardo et al, there appears an excerpt from a taped conversation in which a distinction is made between being "made" and being "proposed" (for membership). The indictment narrative suggests that there is a type or probationary status between the two. In the excerpt, taped on January 12, 1978, Anthony Russo (who has since been murdered) is talking to Pat and Vito who have apparently been proposed for membership in the Genovese family:

In other words, as far as you're concerned, and as far as Vito's concerned . . . when you're proposed it's just like being . . . in other words, I can sit down with made guys and talk about you, and talk in front of you. Unless it's somethin' very, very, important. Then I got to say "Excuse me." But everything else, everybody knows you're proposed.

Reuter and Rubinstein (1978b) write that

It's clear that membership confers certain rights and obligations, but there is disagreement over whether it is better to be a member or a close associate; associates appear to enjoy most of the rights and incur none of the obligations. Which family one joins has relevance apparently only in cases of disputes. There are no restrictions on whom one does business with, but if there is a dispute each member is required to align with his own family. (P. 63)

Reuter and Rubinstein identify one of the advantages of membership — the member has a family to back him up in the case of a dispute. (We will see an example of this in Chapter 7.) An associate in a dispute with a made guy is at a distinct disadvantage. When the associate is a big money-maker, some accommodation may be made. Otherwise, the associate may be in big trouble — trouble that can cost him a beating or even his life. A portion of the "De Cavalcante Tapes" deals with the rights of membership. De Cavalcante (D) is talking to Angelo Bruno (B), Philadelphia crime family boss.* Jimmy, a member of Bruno's family, is feuding with Gnatz, a member of de Cavalcante's family.

B: Sam, look, Sam. Let's say this thing goes to arguimendo, which I don't want it to go.
D: I don't either.
B: I don't want it to go, you understand. If it goes to arguimendo, I have to represent Jimmy whether I want to or not, and so does he. You understand, we have to represent him to the best of our ability without lying and without taking advantage of you. Now if we go to their arguimendo, you understand, and your representando is there and let's say a few other representandos are there, because he ain't going to make the decision and I ain't going to make the decision. Other people are going to make the decision, you're right. I mean, first, first it would be Nick and I, Gnatz, he is under you. We get together and talk about it. We can't get together, it has to go further. It goes out of our hands. It just can't lay like that. It's got to go out of our hands. When it goes out of our hands, then they make the decision. Now we have to represent Jimmy with the right thing. You understand?

---

*On March 21, 1980, Angelo Bruno, age 69, was killed with a single shotgun blast while he sat in a car in front of his modest house in south Philadephia, a predominantly working-class Italian neighborhood. Bruno was born in Sicily, and his only jail term was for refusing to answer questions before the New Jersey State Commission of Investigation in 1973 (Schumacher, 1980, p. 16). According to federal officials Bruno's murder was ordered by Frank ("Funzi") Tieri, boss of the Genovese family (discussed in Chapter 6).

A major disadvantage of membership is suggested by Teresa (1973):

When you're made by the Office   name of organized crime in New England they own you, body and soul. They more or less own you as long as you're on the street working for them anyway, but at least you have a chance to refuse to do something when you're not made. . . .

This means that if the Office told you that your kid   not necessarily referring to a son but to someone close   was out of line, go whack him in the head – if you don't, they whack you and him out. That's how a lot of mob hits are set up. They use a man's relative, his best friend to set him up.

ROLES

Cressey (1969) has stressed the importance of specialists in organized crime families, persons filling functional roles. They may be members or associates, and Cressey offers four such permanent roles. Without the presence of two of these roles (enforcer and corrupter), he argues, you do not have organized crime.

1. Enforcer. He is a penal administrator, a "warden" who arranges for the imposition of a penalty – death. He is an expeditor acting under orders from superiors. He has no authority to punish or make decisions about punishment. He carries out decisions through persons he has available, who have the role of executioner. It is not clear if the enforcer is always a member, or if he can be an associate.

2. Executioner. As the title indicates, he has a specialty, the ability to perform impersonal acts of violence with a great deal of skill. According to Teresa (1973), the New England family of Raymond Patriarca used non-Italian executioners.

3. Money-mover. He is a kind of treasurer who works for the family or some part of it – an expert in financial matters who goes into a vague kind of partnership with any family member who needs his expertise. He has the ability to put large sums of illicit money into legitimate areas while hiding its real ownership.

4. Corrupter. He nullifies "the law enforcement and political processes primarily by outright bribery and other rationally designed forms of 'influence' such as contributions to political campaigns and promises to deliver votes in a particular area" (Cressey, 1969, p. 271).

In Chapter 7 we will be exposed to another role, the paperman.

The literature does not offer evidence of the functional roles as being either fixed or fluid. Ianni (1972) states that the evidence of the existence of enforcers in the family (related by blood or marriage in this case) he studied is weak (p. 115). However, two members of that family could be seen as fulfilling the corrupter role (p. 114), while another with business acumen could be said to fulfill a money-mover role.

RULES

Cresey (1967a) believes that "the fundamental basis of any government, legal or illegal, is a code of conduct. Government structure is always closely associated with the code of behavior which its members are expected to follow" (p. 40). However, he admits, "We have been unable to locate even a summary of the code of conduct which is used in governing the lives of American criminal 'families'" (p. 41). This deficiency is corrected by assuming commonality between the code of prison inmates and that or organized crime.

> The snippets of information we have been able to obtain have convinced us that there is a striking similarity between the code of conduct and the enforcement machinery used in the confederation of organized criminals and the code of conduct and enforcement machinery which governs the behavior of prisoners. This is no coincidence for, as indicated earlier, both the prisoner government and the confederation government are responses to strong official governments which are limited in their means for achieving their control objectives. In order to maintain their status as governors of illegal organizations, the leaders of the two types of organization must promulgate and enforce similar behavior codes. (P. 41)

Based on this analogy, Cressey (1969) provides five rules of conduct.

1. Be loyal to members of the organization. Do not interfere with each other's interests. Do not be an informer.
2. Be rational. Be a member of the team. Do not engage in battle if you cannot win.
3. Be a man of honor. Always do right. Respect womanhood and your elders. Do not rock the boat.
4. Be a stand-up guy. Keep your eyes and ears open and your mouth shut. Do not sell out.
5. Have class. Be independent. Know your way around the world (pp. 175-76).

SUMMARY OF ISSUE TWO

There is evidence that member status differs from associate status in Italian-American organized crime. The literature, however, does not offer much in the way of explaining the advantages and disadvantages of each status. There is lack of agreement over the existence of functional roles; while Cressey offers several roles, Ianni fails to find them in the family he studied. Finally, what are the operating rules in organized crime? Cressey, on the basis of "snippets of information," offers the "code of prisoners," which he argues is analogous to the rules of organized crime.

4

The Business of Organized Crime

The Task Force on Organized Crime (1967) contends that the core of organized crime is the business of supplying illegal goods and services desired by millions (p. 1). The task force lists these goods and services (pp. 2-5):

1. Gambling. Gambling is described as "the greatest source of revenue for organized crime" (p. 2), a view challenged by Reuter and Rubinstein (1977, 1978a, 1978b). This service includes lotteries ("numbers"), book-making, and casino-type gambling.

2. Loan sharking. Loan sharking is described as "the second largest source of income for organized crime" (Task Force on Organized Crime, 1967, p. 3).

3. Narcotics. This area includes the importation and wholesale-level trafficking in controlled substances.

4. Other goods and services. These include prostitution and bootlegging, both of which, the task force notes, have declined in importance One might add pornography to this category.

5. Labor racketeering. Although not necessarily a good or a service, except in the broadest sense, the task force notes that labor racketeering is a source of income for organized crime: "Control of labor supply and infiltration of labor unions by organized crime prevent unionization of some industries, provide opportunities for stealing from union funds and extorting money by threats of possible labor strife, and provide funds from the enormous union pension and welfare systems for business ventures controlled by organized criminals" (p. 5).

6. Business and industrial racketeering. The task force does not discuss this business of organized crime, which was discussed in Chapter 1 and will be discussed in Chapters 7 and 8. It involves two basic approaches – outright extortion (the "protection" racket) or actual protection from unrestrained

29

competition, a service that may be provided at the request of (otherwise) legitimate entrepreneurs.

7. Miscellaneous services. These include financing and/or providing other services, (for example, information) to illegal operators, often predatory criminals such as burglars and robbers. This aspect of organized crime is often overlooked (and is by the task force) and will be discussed in Chapters 7 and 8. Other services include scams (planned bankruptcies used to defraud suppliers; see De Franco 1973), arson, fencing of stolen goods (see Walsh 1977), smuggling untaxed cigarettes (see Gasper 1969), and counterfeiting of records, tapes, and the like.

Schelling (1971) is critical of the goods-and-services argument. He states that the core of organized crime activity is monopolized extortion. Thus, the purveyors of the goods and services are actually the victims of organized crime. The bookmaker, lottery operator, and the loan shark are "taxed" by what is generally referred to as organized crime but, Schelling insists, is actually organized extortion – the "protection" racket. This is vividly portrayed in an incident reported by Albert Seedman (1974), former chief of detectives in New York City. A conversation was taped between "Woody," who had swindled $500,000 from Mays Department Store in Brooklyn, and Carmine ("The Snake") Persico, an enforcer for, and in 1980 the reputed boss of, the Profaci crime family. Woody wants to know why he is being "asked" to pay a rather large share of the money he had stolen to Persico who played no part in the scheme. In this excerpt (which I have shortened) Persico replies:

When you get a job with the telephone company, or maybe even Mays Department Store, they take something out of every paycheck for taxes, right?

Right (Woody responds).

Now why, you may ask, does the government have the right to make you pay taxes? The answer to that question Woody is that you pay taxes for the right to live and work and make money at a legit business. Well, it's the exact same situation – you did a crooked job in Brooklyn; you worked hard and earned a lot of money. Now you have got to pay your taxes on it just like in the straight world. Why? Because we let you do it. We're the government. (Mays is in territory dominated by the Profaci family.)

Schelling argues, however, that it is not burglars or robbers or even swindlers who are subjected to organized extortion but those relatively fixed purveyors of illegal goods and services – for example, bookmakers and certain legitimate operators who are susceptible to extortion such as owners of bars, laundries, and refuse collection firms. He states that organized crime works to limit or control market entry, suppress competition, and tax illegal and, at times, legal entrepreneurs. It provides a government where otherwise there would be none and, Schelling argues, where none would be needed – it is forced upon its victims. Thus, Salvatore ("Sally Crash") Panico allegedly forced Manhattan brothel owners to pay "protection" money. In 1980 Panico, a notorious organized crime figure who I once supervised on parole, threatened an FBI agent posing as a brothel owner and was subsequently arrested. The FBI states that Panico controlled a territory that ran from the Upper East Side to the southern end of Manhattan (Post, 1981).

A final area of profit for organized crime is in legitimate business. One of the apparently popular activities of government officials (the task force is no exception) who often provide the grist for journalistic mills has been to decry the infiltration of organized crime into legitimate business. Maltz (1975) points out that "the alternative to penetration of legitimate business is the reinvestment of the ill-gotten gains into the same criminal enterprises, which may cause greater social harm" (p. 83).* A. Anderson (1977) states, however, that funds from illegal business enterprises cannot easily be "profitably reinvested in illegal market enterprises without aggressive expansion of the territory controlled by the group" (p. 77). She notes that members of organized crime may be in the position of having an oversupply of illegal funds that they cannot profitably use to expand illegal activities. Anderson devotes Chapter 6 to this issue and reports on the various reasons for organized crime involvement in legitimate business: establishment of a tax cover, support for illegal market enterprises (providing a legitimate front for an illegal business), providing services to members (for example, jobs for members and their relatives without the risk of arrest, for probationers, and for parolees), diversification to reduce the risks associated with illegal business ventures, and profit. Anderson notes that one of the important reasons for organized crime members being involved in legitimate business appears to be the security of income that permits the transfer of assets to dependents.

Maltz (1975) suggests that the penetration of organized crime into legitimate business can be viewed as the equivalent to the legitimation of family fortunes by the "robber barons" of an earlier era (p. 83). As proof of "ethnic succession" in organized crime, Ianni (1972) stresses the movement of the Lupollos (a pseudonym) out of organized crime and into legitimate activities.

---

*In the last chapter, Anthony Russo, in an excerpt from the "De Cavalcante Tapes," noted that his family is fortunate in having legitimate things for members to earn a living – the alternatives, according to the excerpt, are burglary, holdups, and narcotics trafficking. Russo was murdered on April 29, 1979 in his Long Branch, New Jersey home.

In 1970, forty-two fourth-generation members of the Lupollo-Salemi-Alcamo-Tucci family could be identified. Their movement towards legitimation seems almost complete. Only four of the twenty-seven males we traced are involved in the family business. Even when their fathers are active in the family business, most of the children are in legitimate enterprises. (P. 76)

Ianni concludes that

contact with those fourth-generation members who did remain in the family business revealed their feeling that by the next generation the Lupollos will have completed their transition from the Italian-American community into American society, and, if allowed, will complete the process of legitimation which old Giuseppe (founding patriarch) started in the 1920s (when he began moving into legitimate business). (P. 83)

SUMMARY OF ISSUE THREE

There is disagreement over the business of organized crime: Is it essentially a provider of illegal goods and services or merely an extorter from those who provide them? The literature pays little or no attention to the role of organized crime in conventional criminal activities such as robbery, burglary, and so on. Finally, is organized crime a threat to legitimate business?

PART 2

The Study

5

Defining Organized Crime

In researching organized crime, one is faced with the task of defining the phenomenon. Oddly enough, a great many works on the subject avoid this issue. Landesco (1968) does not provide a definition, nor does A. Anderson (1979). In an issue of the Annals (Tyler 1963), which consists of 12 articles on organized crime, no definition is offered. Bequai (1979) spends six pages defining organized crime, but he fails to define it. Homer (1974) spends 14 pages discussing the definition of organized crime and then fails to provide a succinct (it takes 8 pages) definition. Paradoxically, the Organized Crime Control Act of 1970 does not define organized crime. The Task Force on Organized Crime (1976) never comes to grips with the problem of definition and, instead, proposes a description that attempts to "(1) explain something of the nature of organized crime activity, and (2) dispel stereotypes surrounding organized crime by indicating what it is not" (p. 7, emphasis added). Mack (1973) points out that in Europe organized "takes in all criminal operations, however small-scale, in which more than one person participates and some rudimentary role-differentiation occurs" (p. 103). Thus, in Europe, one does not have organized crime but, instead, criminals with varying degrees of organization, from the primitive to the hierarchical. Mack notes that taken literally, "organized crime" covers "anything other than spur-of-the moment crime" (p. 104).

Cressey (1969), as part of his support for legislative efforts to make participation in organized crime illegal per se, provides a "preliminary legal definition."

> An organized crime is any crime committed by a person occupying in an established division of labor, a position designed for the commission of crime, providing that such division of labor also includes at least one position for a corrupter, one position for a corruptee, and one position for an enforcer. (P. 31)

This is the definition provided by the FBI when asked how they define organized crime. This, of course, is a definition of an organized crime and not of organized crime. Maltz (1975) attempts to deal with this problem of semantics.

Central to the lack of consistent definitions is a semantic problem. The word "crime" is usually taken to mean the aggregate of specific "crimes"; i.e., a crime is a specific behavior or act, and crime is the set of behaviors encompassing all crimes. In like manner we can call an organized crime a specific behavior or act. Yet when we talk of organized crime in the generic sense we usually refer, not to a set of behaviors, but to an entity, a group of (unspecified) people, a disease, a bogeyman. For example, we read headlines such as "Organized Crime Controls the Scavenger Industry in Westchester," "The Penetration of Legitimate Business by Organized Crime," "Why Organized Crime Thrives," and other anthropomorphisms. (P. 74)

Maltz offers a "tentative definition/typology" of organized crime.

A crime consists of a transaction proscribed by criminal law between offender(s) and victim(s). It is not necessary for the victim to be a complainant or to consider himself victimized for a crime to be committed. An organized crime is a crime in which there is more than one offender, and the offenders are and intend to remain associated with one another for the purpose of committing crimes. The means of executing the crime include violence, theft, corruption, economic power, deception, and victim collusion or participation. These are not mutually ·exclusive categories; any organized crime may employ a number of these means.
    The objective of most organized crimes is power, either political or economic. These types of objectives, too, are not mutually exclusive and may exist in any organized crime.
    There are a number of manifestations the objectives may take. When the objective is political power, it may be of two types: overthrow of the existing order, or illegal use of the criminal process. When the objective is economic power, it may manifest itself in three different ways: through common crime (mala in se), through illegal business (mala prohibita or "vices"), or through legitimate business (white-collar crime). (P. 76)

Maltz stresses means, objectives, and manifestations — organization and role differentiation are omitted. His definition/typology does not provide an adequate basis for distinguishing between the James Gang (of Wild West fame) and the Capone organization (of Prohibition fame). While our predilections permit us to accept Al Capone as an organized crime figure,

Jesse James does not present an intuitively pleasing ideal type. Indeed, while the Capone organization continued (and continues) after his imprisonment and subsequent death, "the killing of America's Jesse James ended his outlawed gang of plunderers" (Cressey, 1972, p. 100).

Albini (1971) defines organized crime "as any activity involving two or more individuals, specialized or non-specialized, encompassing some form of social structure, with some form of leadership, utilizing certain modes of operation, in which the ultimate purpose of the organization is found in the enterprises of the particular group" (p. 37). This broad definition allows Albini to subdivide organized crime and to differentiate organized crime from syndicate crime: organized crime is not necessarily syndicate crime – the former subsumes the latter. Thus, organized crime may include the political – for example, the Ku Klux Klan or Molly Maguires; the mercenary, theft-oriented organizations – for example, the James Gang; and the in-group, outlaw motorcycle gangs – for example, the Hell's Angels (pp. 38-47).

Syndicate organized crime "differs from the other types of organized crime primarily because it provides goods and/or services that are illegal, yet for which there is a demand by certain elements of society" (p. 47). This form of organized crime and the other forms proposed by Albini are problematic. If providing goods and services is crucial, Hell's Angels and other outlaw motorcycle gangs may have to be moved into the syndicate category. According to local officials, motorcycle gangs have gained a monopoly over the distribution of certain controlled substances, particularly methamphetamine hydrochloride, in areas of North Carolina. There have been similar reports in California and Ohio. An April 1980 report by the Office of Intelligence of the United States Drug Enforcement Administration (U.S., Drug Enforcement Administration) reports, "By virtually every standard, outlaw motorcycle gangs are organized crime groups" of the syndicate type (p. 15). Jesse James, on the other hand, was viewed as a political actor by midwestern farmers "because he typically limited his exploits to the robbery of banks and railroads – institutions hated by Jesse's worshippers" (Inciardi, Block, and Hallowell, 1977, p. 73). Lasswell and McKenna (1972) distinguish between organized crime and politically oriented organized crime: (regular) organized crime is nonideological in its perspectives (p. 24).

Syndicate criminals have often engaged in rather predatory criminal activity that does not seem based on a concept of goods and services – bank robbery, for example, for which the prominent New York syndicate criminal John ("Sonny") Franzese (of the Colombo family) was imprisoned for eight years. Charles ("Chuckie") Crimaldi, an executioner for the Chicago syndicate ("The Outfit"), reports that he continued his involvement in armed robbery even after he had an established position in syndicate crime. Crimaldi states that his continued involvement in such activity was only in part for money; mostly, he avers, it was for excitement (Kidner, 1976). On December 11, 1978, six men robbed the Lufthansa Airlines cargo terminal in

Kennedy Airport for $5.8 million, the largest cash haul in U.S. history. Early newspaper reports indicated that the robbery gang had been responsible for numerous thefts and hijackings in Queens and Brooklyn and was reputed to be associated with Paul Vario of the Lucchese family. Feiden (1979) reports Vario allegedly arranged the operation, inside information for the robbery being furnished by a Lufthansa employee who was in debt to a syndicate bookmaker (p. 37). Several of the participants have been murdered, others are standing trial, and at least one is in protective custody. The organized crime connection appears to be accurate.

Two crucial variables for the definition of <u>organized crime</u> that will be used in this study are time and monopoly. Several definitions stress the first variable: self-perpetuating conspiracy or intricate conspiracies carried on over many years; or persistence of the conspiracy through time or the intent that the conspiracy should persist through time. Schelling (1971) stresses the second variable; he refers to organized crime as monopoly crime, and Whyte (1961) notes the need to limit competition: "The syndicate operates to stifle outside competition" (p. 117). This is done by superior organization that is operationalized through political and police protection and the exercise of "muscle" – coercion through violence including murder (p. 120). Ianni (1972) reports that the Lupollos control gambling in sections of Brooklyn and Long Island: "In gambling the territorial control is complete, and no 'independent' can operate very long without some difficulty either from the police or the Lupollos, or both" (p. 98). Salerno and Tompkins (1969) state that the most valuable advantage of organized crime "is a thing that ordinary businessmen dream about, and sometimes go to jail for trying to arrange: the absence of competition" (p. 186).

To distinguish the term <u>organized crime</u> as it is used in this study from other posible definitions, I will offer the following (Abadinsky, 1981):

> A nonideological enterprise that involves a number of persons in close social interaction, organized on a hierarchical basis for the purpose of securing profit and power* by engaging in illegal and legal activities that yield high profits while offering relatively low risks. Positions are assigned on the basis of kinship or rationally assigned according to skill. Positions are continuous and not dependent on the

---

*<u>Power</u> is another term that presents problems of definition. See, for example, Bacherach and Lawler (1976) and Wrong (1968). To maintain internal consistency with the need for definition, I will use the following definition of <u>power</u>: "the probability that one actor within a social relationship will be a position to carry out his own will despite resistance, regardless of the basis on which this probability rests" (Weber, 1968, p. 53).

individuals occupying them at any particular time. There is a permanency assumed by the members who strive to keep the enterprise integral and active in pursuit of its goals. It eschews competition and strives for monopoly over particular activities on an industrial or territorial basis. There is a willingness to use violence and/or bribery to achieve ends or maintain discipline. Membership is restricted, although nonmembers are involved on a contingency basis.

6

Methodological Problems

It is axiomatic that the further away one is situated from the source of data, the greater the questions of reliability and validity – the truth and accuracy of the data. This is a particularly acute problem in studying organized crime where indirect sources abound. Block (1978) notes that when it comes to organized crime, there is a reliance on unsubstantiated accounts of informers or the ideological preoccupations of law enforcement agencies (p. 470). Galliher and Cain (1974) point out that there is a lack of scholarly material relating to organized crime, with the dominant literature being journalistic, and tending toward sensationalism, or government documents: "There are two troublesome aspects to this reliance on such sources, one empirical, the other political. In arriving at conclusions and statements of fact, the journalist or political investigator is not bound by the canons of scientific investigation as is the social scientist" (p. 73). This is made poignant by Villano (1978) an FBI agent for 23 years, who writes that the bureau regularly released false reports to stir up dissension among organized crime figures (pp. 246-47).

In 1974 a book written by Gosch and Hammer, the latter a former reporter for the New York Times, that purported to be the Last Testament of Lucky Luciano, was published: "Dictated by Charles 'Lucky' Luciano himself during the final months of his life." The book's introduction explains that Luciano made a decision in 1961 to provide the details of his life as a crime boss to Gosch, a motion picture producer (p. v). According to the introduction, the syndicate, acting on orders from Meyer Lansky, vetoed a movie that Gosch was producing, The Lucky Luciano Story. Luciano, who was living in exile in Italy, was to be technical adviser, and now he was angry. However, according to Gosch, who died of a heart attack before publication, Luciano extracted a promise that his autobiography not be published earlier than ten years after his death; he died in 1962. The book earned $1 million before it was even published, and paperback rights were auctioned off for an additional $800,000 (Gage, 1974, p. 1).

On December 17, 1974, in a front page article, Nicholas Gage of the New York Times questioned the authenticity of the book by pointing to numerous errors of fact: "It is widely known that Mr. Gosch met on a number of occasions with Mr. Luciano on the aborted film project, and presumably the gangster recounted some of his experiences during these meetings. But, contradictions and inaccuracies in the book raise questions to the claim that Mr. Luciano told his whole life to Mr. Gosch and that everything in the book attributed to Mr. Luciano actually came from him" (p. 28). For example, there is the question of Luciano's nickname, "Lucky." Gosch and Hammer attribute it to Luciano's survival after being beaten and left for dead during the Castellammarese War. However, there are newspaper reports that show Luciano was known as "Lucky" prior to the incident. ("Lucky" is probably derived from his real surname Lucania.)

The problem inherent in securing accurate data about organized crime is highlighted by events surrounding the murder of Salvatore Maranzano (discussed in Chapter 1). Maranzano was killed on September 10, 1931. Cressey (1969) reports that "on that day and the two days immediately following, some forty Italian-Sicilian gang leaders across the country lost their lives in battle" (p. 44). Cook (1972) refers to this episode as the "Purge of the Greasers": "Within a few short hours, the old-time crime bosses who had been born and reared in Sicily and were mostly illiterate – the 'Mustache Petes' or 'the greasers,' as they were sometimes called – were liquidated by the new breed of Americanized, business-oriented gangsters of the Luciano-Costello-Adonis school." Cook adds that "beginning on September 11th and lasting throughout the next day, some thirty to forty executions were performed across the nation" (p. 108). A special edition of New York Magazine adds to the story: "During the bloodbath nearly 40 of the Old Guard were executed in various ingenious ways" (Plate, 1972, p. 45, emphasis added).

Block (1978) surveyed newspapers in eight major cities, beginning with issues two weeks prior to Maranzano's death ending two weeks after, looking for stories of gangland murders that could be connected, even remotely, with the Maranzano case. He reports, "While I found various accounts of the Maranzano murder, I could locate only three murders that might have been connected" (p. 460). As he notes, three murders do not make a "purge." Block suggests that "it is by no means clear why so many scholars have bought a story which so grossly violates historical respectability" (Inciardi, Block, and Hallowell, 1977, p. 100). Nelli (1976) reports that the purge believed by criminal informants in New York to have taken place nationwide "applied only to that city and (the murders) were not repeated elsewhere" (p. 182). Actually, the purge account lacks internal credibility. The murder of some 40 top Sicilian gangsters within a 48-hour period appears quite outrageous for several reasons. First, as noted in Chapter 1, it took at least four men impersonating law enforcement officers to kill Maranzano, and many more had to know of the plot. To kill 40 tough Sicilian gangsters who were often armed, cautious, and accompanied by trusted bodyguards would have required a conspiracy involving hundreds of persons. Second, if only one person informed, which, given the Byzantine nature of organized crime, is likely, the purge would have been aborted with serious consequences – the proposed victims would have gone into hiding and most likely would have struck back preemptively at the plotters. Luciano would have recognized these problems, even if Cressey and the others did not. Nelli states that a nationwide purge was unnecessary: "In the Maranzano case the message stated clearly that any oldtimers still permitted to live had better accept and adjust to the new order" (p. 182).

D. Smith (1975) points to an American "preoccupation with conspiracy." One of the conditions required for an "alien conspiracy theory" is a set of "facts" or assumptions that can be constructed into evidence supporting a conspiratorial explanation (p. 77). These facts often make fascinating reading, they sell newspapers and books, and, Smith argues, they provided the Federal Bureau of Narcotics with an explanation for failure: "The notion of total suppression of illegal narcotics use through importation control was a self-proclaimed mission, and it had not been attained. How better to explain failure (and, incidentally, to prepare the ground for increased future budgets) than to argue that, dedicated though it might be, the bureau was hard pressed to overcome an alien, organized, conspiratorial force which, with evil intent and conspiratorial methods, had forced its way on an innocent public"? (P. 85) •

That the federal narcotics agency, now called the Drug Enforcement Administration, is still capable of the type of activities noted by Smith is made apparent by a 1977 episode. In one week major stories (Meskil (1977) and Franks (1977)) appeared revealing that Carmine Galente ("Lilo"), boss of the Bonanno family, was emerging as the capo di tutti capi, the "boss of bosses." Meskil (1977), an investigative reporter who has written extensively on organized crime, stated that law enforcement officials say that Galente's immediate goal is to bring all five New York families under his control, and according to these officials, he will succeed: "Soon, federal agents predict, Carmine Galente's peers on the Mafia Commission will elect him boss of all bosses" (p. 28). Franks (1977), a Pulitzer Prize winning reporter for the New York Times, wrote that "officials say that Mr. Galente is moving to merge the five New York crime families under his own leadership and aims to become a national chieftain who would try to restore the Mafia to a position of power that it has not held in at least 20 years" (p. 34).

Capeci (1978) reports, however, that the real "Godfather" is actually Frank ("Funzi") Tieri,* the 74-year-old boss of the Genovese family. Capeci

_____

*On January 24, 1981, the 76-year-old Tieri received a 10-year federal sentence. He is the first person ever convicted of being the boss of a crime family. The conviction was made possible by the Racketeer Influenced and

contends that Galente was being proclaimed boss of all bosses as "the result of a well-planned 'leak' by the Drug Enforcement Administration of a 'confidential' report by its Unified Intelligence Division" (p. 28). Capeci adds, "It turns out that the report was based on quite old information and was leaked in self-interest by the drug agency." The federal narcotics agency had been succesful in convicting Galente (and Genovese as well) of narcotic law violations in 1962. If Galente now emerged as boss of bosses, this success would take on new significance. However, if there is a "Mafia Commission," they apparently decided not to "anoint" Galente — on July 12, 1979, several heavily armed men entered an Italian restaurant in Brooklyn and dispatched the would-be capo di tutti capi.

ORGANIZED CRIME RESEARCH USING GOVERNMENT DOCUMENTS

Cressey (1967b) states that "basic methodological problems stem from the fact the society of organized criminals, if it is a society, is a secret society. The ongoing activities of organized criminals are not accessible to observation by the ordinary citizen or the ordinary social scientist" (p. 102, emphasis added). Cressey reports that "an organization of 'organized criminals' exists, but it must be studied by methods not ordinarily utilized by social scientists" (p. 102). These methods actually boil down to using data from government sources, hardly a novel approach. However, Cressey maintains that they are not ordinarily utilized by social scientists because when it comes to organized crime "one must have 'connections,' such as appointment as a consultant to the President's Commission." Cressey acknowledges that

> The principal handicap here stems from the fact that there are no "hard data" on organized crime. The information in the files of law-enforcement and investigative agencies, even those whose principal function is the assembling of intelligence information, is by no means oriented to providing assistance to social science theorists. As indicated above, law-enforcement agencies are necessarily concerned wih apprehending and convicting individual criminals, and questions that social scientists would have them ask simply do not occur. Further, informants are not available for interview, and there is no known way to observe the everyday interactions of organized criminals with each other, with other criminals, or with noncriminals. These facts of life pose serious methodological problems for the social

Corrupt Organizations (RICO) section of the Organized Crime Control Act of 1970. RICO imposes sanctions on racketeers based not only the crime they commit, but on their status as racketeers.

scientist who would learn something about the norms, values, and rules of organized criminal society, because such phenomena are social-psychological in nature and, therefore, are readily observable only in the context of interaction. (P. 109)

A. Anderson (1979), like Cressey, had "connections" as a Visiting Fellow with the National Institute of Law Enforcement and Criminal Justice. For her doctoral dissertation she studied one organized crime family using government data:

> The primary sources for this study were provided by a federal agency. The data were gathered during spring and summer 1970 by abstracting information from government reports. The information as presented in these reports is neither organized nor analyzed. A particular report (of which there were hundreds) might include information on a number of matters – an illegal market operation, ownership of a legitimate business, membership in the group – with no cross-referencing to other reports where the same matters are considered. A great deal of sorting out and collating was therefore necessary. Occasional documents summarizing information from the reports were available, but like the reports themselves, the information they offer is descriptive and factual; no estimates or projections are made and no conclusions drawn. (P. 149)

She reports that informants "provided a significant portion of the information available in the data sources," and she adds that "the information they provide is not necessarily accurate" and that the informants are not identified so that "the internal consistency of information provided by a particular informant" could not be determined. Anderson attempted to deal with this problem by not including informant information in the data base unless it was verified by another source or informant (p. 150). She notes that at times the statements of informants were contradictory. To supplement her information, Anderson interviewed federal and state law enforcement officials and private citizens concerned with the problem of organized crime. These included members of private consulting firms involved in projects bearing on organized crime and reporters for news media who specialized in organized crime reporting (p. 151).

Interestingly, although the same basic sources were used, Anderson comes to a different (more benign) conclusion about organized crime than did Cressey. For this reason, D. Smith (1980b), in a review of Anderson's work, is inclined to believe her despite some methodological misgivings: "My inclination to believe Anderson is rooted in considerable measure in the fact that her analysis refutes a great deal of what has been said before" (p. 100). Smith writes

The sticking point may be Anderson's evidence, which cannot be identified and must therefore be taken on faith. I am inclined to believe in her scholarly intent and integrity, but I must confess to my lack of patience with the euphemism "a federal agency" as her source. (Pp. 99-100)

Perhaps the most insightful statement about using government sources for researching organized crime was made by Reuter and Rubinstein (1978b).

The difficulty the government had in obtaining information on the reserves of energy-producing companies in the wake of the 1973 oil boycott should serve as a sober reminder of how difficult it is to collect accurate information even from legitimate organizations operating in a highly regulated environment. The challenges are immeasurably greater in collecting information about people who are consciously involved in illegal activities. (P. 57)

ORGANIZED CRIME RESEARCH USING ETHNOGRAPHY AND PARTICIPANT OBSERVATION

Ianni (1974) reveals that during his 1972 study of the Lupollos he discovered that "ethnic succession" was continuing in organized crime – in this instance, blacks and Hispanics replacing Italians (p. 341). However, there was a problem for Ianni in researching this phenomenon.

The foundation for all anthropological field work lies in the complex relationship between the anthropologist and his informants. His task and skill are in describing the social behavior of a people as exactly, as meaningfully and as intelligibly as possible. To do so requires that he understand their life style in a way that approaches their own definition of reality. As a result, it is essential that he establish a really satisfactory and amicable relationship with the people among whom he is going to live. All of these conditions were in my favor when I studied the Lupollos. I shared their ethnicity, spoke their language and knew them even before I began the study. (P. 343)

None of this would be true in studying black and Hispanic groups involved in organized criminal activities.

Ianni dealt with this problem by using field assistants, indigenous "street people," often with criminal records. They were trained in observation and recording techniques. Besides the personnel problems encountered by using such marginal works (for example, some were drug addicts who returned to drug use), there was the problem of credibility.

A major question for me throughout the research and one that must have struck the reader, is, given the nature of the research and means by which the data were gathered, how is it possible to assess the reliability or truth and the validity or accuracy of the information presented here. Reliability and validity are age-old problems in field research but they were particular problems here because we were using informants as observers so that the data were always one step removed from my own control and experience. Our solution was to establish a standardized system of assessing both the validity of the data we were gathering and the reliability of the individuals who were gathering it. This system, which I had used previously in studying the Lupollos, is based upon separate judgments of how reliable each informant is and what evidence – documentation, my own checking out of the information, internal consistency and corroboration by other informants – there is that any particular piece of datum he is reporting is accurate or valid. (P. 348)

Fisher (1975), in a review of Ianni's work, is highly critical of his methodology. Instead of methodological constraint and rigor, Fisher argues, Ianni's work is thoroughly infused with "fill-ins," as if to round out a story with creative and suggestive imaginings (p. 84).* He accuses Ianni of "flights of fancy and ungrounded interpretation" (p. 85). He also questions how Ianni was able to study so wide a variety of criminal activity in so short a time (18 months).

Whyte (1961) dealt with the methodogical issues raised by Cressey back in 1937, although he did not set out to study organized crime per se. Using participant observation, Whyte was able to show that if organized crime is a secret society, in Cornerville at least, it was a rather open secret society. Whyte, an upper-middle-class Harvard graduate student, had a background far removed from the life in Cornerville (p. 280). Yet, he is able to provide data on organized crime in an Italian ghetto. Chambliss (1975) reports on the (apparent) ease with which he was able to uncover details of organized crime in Seattle:

So I went to the skid row, Japanese, Filipino, and Black sections of Seattle dressed in truck driver's clothes. Within three days I dis-

---

*Tyler, in a review of Ianni's work, questions Ianni's conclusions. He notes that the evidence "consists of a pimp with a stable of seven hookers, a dope pusher, a fence who dabbles in loan sharking and gambling, a con man who gets phony insurance policies for gypsy cabs, and a numbers racketeer, etc. (1975: 178)." Although these activities are organized, Tyler notes "they are not in a class with white organized crime either qualitatively or quantitatively (Ibid.)," and thus not supportive of a theory of "ethnic succession."

covered that widespread gambling, prostitution, drug trafficking, and pornography distribution were being completely ignored by the police, while white drunks on skid row and Black teenagers in the ghetto were being regularly busted. (Pp. 36-37)

After two months of talking informally to people he met at various card games, Chambliss "decided it was time 'to blow my cover,' " and he revealed his position at the university. Through the manager of a card room Chambliss was able to interview many persons with knowledge of organized crime: "And there was one honest-to-god clandestine meeting in a deserted warehouse down at the wharf" (p. 38). Chambliss reports that

Over the next ten years I pursued this inquiry, widening my contacts and participating in an ever larger variety of rackets. As my interests in these subjects and my reliability as someone who could be trusted spread, I received more offers to "talk" than I had time to pursue.

Whyte, in a forward to Ianni's (1972) work, points out that Ianni was able to penetrate deeper into organized crime than he could in Cornerville (p. xi). Ianni is the son of an Italian immigrant family from Abruzzi, well north of Naples. However, he lived among southern Italians, Neapolitans, and Sicilians during his formative years in the "Little Italy" of Wilmington, Delaware (pp. 175-76). Ianni was director of research programs in the U.S. Office of Education. One day he met Phil Alcamo in the office of a congressman. Phil was his entry into the Lupollo family (p. 178). Unlike Whyte's relationship with Doc, the friendship between Ianni and Alcamo "was based principally on co-ethnicity" (p. 179). Ianni notes that his status as a university professor (at the time of the study) made him somewhat unusual in the Lupollo network that included businessmen and professionals as well as crime family operatives, "but my background as an Italian-American made me an accepted member of the group. I moved freely and easily in this world, which centers around a few social and athletic clubs and a number of Italian restaurants. I could enter the network at any time by going to one of the clubs or restaurants" (p. 181).

During his three years of field study, Ianni did move in and out of the network, and he notes that

Because of the nature of this study, however, there were some additional problems. In the first place, the group I was observing was a closed system, at least part of which — the illegal activities — I could not hope to observe with any degree of regularity. I could not really immerse myself in the lives of the people I was studying and had to be content with observing whenever the opportunity presented itself. (P. 180)

The major shortcoming of Ianni's work is that "it did not lead him into intimate contact with illegal activities, for he found a degree of specialization and division of labor within the family, and his relations were closest among those largely engaged in 'legitimate' activities" (Whyte's Foreword to Ianni, 1972, p. xii).

Had Ianni been exposed to (at least felonious) criminal activity, he could have been in a potentially difficult legal situation, as would any other scientific or even casual observer. The offense of misprison of felony refers to persons having knowledge of the actual commission of a felony who conceal and do not, as soon as possible, make known the same to the proper authorities. In Whyte's (1961) work we find that he was actually involved in voting frauds. Ned Polsky (quoted in Becker, 1973) argues, "If one is effectively to study law-breaking deviants as they engage in their deviance in its natural settings, i.e., outside of jail, he must make the moral decision that in some ways he will break the law himself" (p. 171).

While it might be suggested that participant observation be used in conjunction with official law enforcement sources, this presents serious methodological problems – problems that preclude using this combination effectively. First, if both sources realize that you are also dealing with their "adversaries," a trusting relationship may be impossible. (Not providing such information would be both unethical and dangerous.) Second, there is an ethical problem: inadvertently disclosing information, perhaps only providing "leads," to one or the other source. This can be done through information-laden questions, for example. Third, given the usual formal and informal interaction between criminal actors and enforcement personnel, the researcher may find that he or she is being used as an intermediary or messenger. Points two and three can cause the researcher to influence events that he or she is supposed to be investigating.

METHODOLOGY USED IN THIS STUDY

There are two traditional ways to research organized crime: through the use of government records and by participant observation. The first has been used by other social scientists with (at best) mixed results. I was precluded from using the second because of my background in law enforcement, which included working in the organized crime areas of Red Hook, Bath Beach, Bensonhurst, and Ridgewood (all in the Borough of Brooklyn). I did not believe that my university affiliation would have provided sufficient credibility for being considered a neutral or benign observer. It was serendipitous that I discovered someone who had been involved with Italian organized crime in, of all places, North Carolina. A search of the literature reveals a number of life histories, the more prominent ones being Shaw (1966) and Sutherland (1972), but there are no life histories dealing with organized crime as defined in Chapter 5.

METHODOLOGICAL PROBLEMS

To prepare for Vito, I immersed myself in a study of organized crime. In addition to the available literature, I was able to persuade the North Carolina Justice Academy, the state training facility for police officers, to permit me to attend their one-week training session on organized crime. Most of the instructors were either from federal enforcement agencies or retired intelligence officers from the New York City Police Department, including Ralph Salerno. I also reviewed all of the information that I could secure about Vito: newspaper stories, one in the New York Times that included his photograph, a short excerpt in a popular book on organized crime, and a briefing from the U.S. marshal (with Vito's permission). Vito's willingness to participate in this study is, at least in part, related to a desire to vent his anger over the Witness Protection Program, which he states treated him poorly. Vito presents a convincing case that the program is inadequate.

The sessions with Vito took place in my home, over coffee and cake. Except for our first meeting, when he came with a rather large, somewhat ominous-looking man (who turned out to be his son-in-law), only Vito and I were present. To structure the sessions without reducing spontaneity, Vito was given a set of questions or topics on a sheet of paper immediately prior to the start of the session – he was handed the questions and the tape recorder was turned on. Nothing in Vito's narrative is contrary to known information about organized crime, nor were they any internal inconsistencies. Vito has transaction immunity and was free to discuss his criminal activities without fear of prosecution. He did not make any (discernible) effort to "clean up" his activities nor to exaggerate his importance in organized crime. For example, after he related his first "big score," I asked how he felt afterward, an obvious opportunity to express remorse even at this late date. "How did I feel about what I had done? Guilty – for all of about three seconds," he said with a smile. When he was privy to some rather high-level meetings, he reports feeling like a "bump of a log," that he had no reason for being present.

When Vito did not have sufficient information to respond adequately to my queries, he would preface his response with: "I don't really know the answer to that, but I could guess." His guesses, while interesting, were not included in the case study. At one point Vito began providing some rather interesting information about the infrastructure of the Gambino and Genovese families; it seems that one important New Jersey crime figure reports to and is affiliated with both families. This, based on what information I had, would be quite unusual. After he finished, I asked how he came to know this information. Vito explained the bits of information that he had encountered and indicated that this had led him to make certain conclusions about the individual's relationship to the two families. He added that his speculation had been "confirmed" by federal authorities. It seems that during a debriefing session in Washington, Justice Department officials left a large wall chart uncovered, from which Vito was able to confirm his speculation. Once again, we must consider the question of data sources; it is conceivable that data are often nothing more than speculation confirmed by speculation. In this instance, the direction of the information is of interest:

informants (?) ———————→ Justice Department ———————→ informant

To maintain confidentiality some names and places have been changed or modified, and some facts about Vito have been omitted even though they may have been of some interest to the reader. I have tried to accomplish an accurate rendition of the taped interviews and have edited the transcribed material only for clarity and continuity. The narrative is as faithful to Vito's own words as I could present and still enable the reader to understand what was said. Soon after the interviews were completed, Vito left North Carolina. I do not know his current whereabouts or the employment that he holds, although we sometimes exchange letters via a post office box from which his mail is forwarded.

The limitations of a life history are obvious; it is, after all, a single case from which conclusions must be carefully drawn before they can be generalized to the larger topic. Howard Becker, in his introduction to Shaw's The Jack Roller: A Delinquent Boy's Own Story (1966), points out the differences between autobiography and life history:

The life history is not conventional social science "data," although it has some of the features of that kind of fact, being an attempt to gather material useful in the formulation of general sociological theory. Nor is it conventional autobiography, although it shares with autobiography its narrative form, its first-person point of view and its frankly subjective stance. (P. v)

Becker notes that

The autobiographer proposes to explain his life to us and thus commits himself to maintaining a close connection between the story he tells and what an objective investigation might discover. When we read autobiography, however, we are always aware that the author is telling us only part of the story, that he has selected his material so as to present us with the picture of himself he would prefer us to have and that he may have ignored what would be trivial or distasteful to him, though of great interest to us.

... the life history is more down to earth, more devoted to our purposes than those of the author, less concerned with artistic values than with a faithful rendering of the subject's experience and interpretation of the world he lives in. The sociologist who gathers a life history takes steps to ensure that it covers everything we want to know, that no important fact or event is slighted, that what purports to be factual squares with other available evidence and that the subject's interpretations are honestly given. The sociologist keeps the subject oriented to the questions sociology is interested in, asks him about events that require amplificiation, tries to make the story told jibe with matters of official record and with material furnished by others familiar with the person, event, or place being described. He keeps the game honest for us. (P. vi)

7
Vito: An Illustrative Case Study

Vito Palermo is approximately 50 years of age, a second-generation American with a southern Italian heritage. He understands Italian, although he does not speak it well. He is married and has several children. Although he was convicted of a crime, he has never served any time in prison. His brother is a college graduate, and Vito is the only member of his family who has ever been involved in criminal activities. He is intelligent and articulate, although his formal education did not extend beyond high school. Since leaving New Jersey Vito has held legitimate positions earning well in excess of what is the usual salary of a full professor. Bracketed footnotes and the other material appearing in brackets are mine; the narrative is Vito's.

My father's refuse company serviced our community and several other surrounding communities. All of the kids that I went to elementary school with were serviced by my father's company, and I became known as the "garbage kid" in school. Kids can be cruel in their way, and it bothered me — it hurt my feelings tremendously. It also resulted in a lot of battles in school, fistfights. We would get out of school at three in the afternoon, and on the way home some kid would say, "Hi garbage." Before you know it we would be rolling all over the ground. I won 90 percent of these bouts and acquired a minor reputation as a tough guy. The end result was that by the time I got out of grammar school, kids were no longer calling me "garbage."

My first disillusionment with law enforcement authority came when I was about 13. The chief of police came to the house and spoke to my father. I was curious about what he wanted, and eavesdropped on the conversation. What the chief wanted was gasoline ration stamps, since this was during the war and gas was rationed. My father received ration stamps as a commercial user in an essential business and always had stamps left over. The chief wanted these stamps. If you knew a guy with a gas station and pulled in with a car using commercial stamps, he would close his eyes to it. My father gave him the stamps, and from that point on he made a weekly call to our house. My mother was concerned that my father was going to get in some kind of trouble. However, if my father had said no to the chief, he could have made business more difficult. As an example, one of my father's trucks would be picking up garbage from the wrong side of the street — driving down the left side to pick up garbarge on a two-way street because there were more houses on that side of the street; the chief could easily order his men to ticket the truck.

A couple of years later I was exposed to a second disillusionment. There was no union for my father's employees, nor was there for his competitor's employees until the Teamsters Union came into the area and opened an office.* The head of the teamster local, the business agent, John Serratelli, interestingly enough, vanished off the face of the earth a number of years ago; they found his Cadillac and no Johnny.†In plain English, John Serratelli turned out to be a real son-of-a-bitch. When he started out organizing the refuse business, he was no more interested in the workers than he was concerned about going to the moon. What he was concerned about was lining his own pockets. Men were being organized without the benefit of knowing it. My father kept their coupon books, paid their dues, without their knowing it, and this, as far as John Serratelli and the Teamsters Union were concerned, showed membership on the books and dues being received. In turn, to make sure that the employees didn't know that they could have an organization or a labor contract, all the refuse contractors bought labor peace by paying John Serratelli off.

My father hated the arrangement, but he had no choice in the matter, because if you didn't conform Johnny would, in fact, organize your men and picket your business, and you are working with a contract with a munici-

---

* Jimmy Hoffa, as part of his campaign to win the presidency of the International Brotherhood of Teamsters (IBT), authorized charters for a number of "paper locals." These charters went to racketeers in exchange for their support at the IBT national convention. See Brill (1978).

† John V. Serratelli was mentioned during the FBI's "Abscam" investigation. He was reputedly an associate of one of the principals, George Katz. According to the New York Times, Serratelli organized a number of garbage contracting companies in New Jersey: "Mr. Serratelli did his organizing with the help of an associate who would throw a lead pipe on the desk of a company owner and say 'These are my credentials.'" The Times noted that in 1959 Serratelli testified at a hearing concerned with the infiltration of organized crime into the refuse business. "Mr. Serratelli, who was indicted for bribery, kept a luncheon date after the hearing ended, and, although his car was found later, he has not been seen since" (Sullivan, 1980, p. 20).

pality where the price is fixed; there were no escalation clauses. You figured your personnel costs when bidding on the contract, and if the cost increased before the contract expired, the contractor had to absorb the loss; this could break a firm.

After high school I began working for my father. He had encouraged me to go to college like my older brother, but I didn't like school. My father made me start at the very bottom of the ladder. I was young and it didn't hurt me in the least to have to throw garbage cans. At the same time he started putting responsibility on my shoulders by giving me the title of "working foreman," which meant more work at the same pay. After high school I married my high school sweetheart, and a year later my first child was born.

When my father lost a contract with a municipality, I lost my job. John Serratelli had double-crossed my father. In addition to the workers, Serratelli had organized the contractors. He would guarantee you, as a contractor, that the work you had would remain yours even under the public bidding procedure. The contractors, under his guidance, would respect each other's jobs. When a contract expired, there would be no competitive bidding, and the contractor would get his price. The theory was that it is better to have one good paying contrct than two mediocre ones. If you disobeyed, Serratelli would pull your men out on strike for higher wages; this was a hell of an incentive. For this service Serratelli would get 3 percent of the gross of the job right off the top. If the job was going to pay, if the contract indicated that the municipality was going to pay let's say $100,000 a year to have their garbage removed and disposed of, you had to pay Serratelli $3,000 right off the top. A local job that had been promised to my father — it had been his for many years — was underbid by another contractor. Serratelli offered all kinds of excuses but did nothing. My father had three other municipal contracts, but there were no real openings for me, and I didn't want him to keep me because I was his son.

I went to work for Joe (we will call him) Adamo as a truck driver. Joe had numerous accounts, and it was my job to go to these accounts and pick up scrap material, various metals, and bring them back to the shop. This was very hard work because Adamo didn't believe in hand trucks; everything was mule work. I worked at this job for about a year and a half. It was while working for Adamo that I made my first very good-sized score by beating my employer out of some money. I had been introduced to a guy named Mattie Brown, and he was as phony as his name. He had been in and out of jail for all kinds of scams, cons, and what have you. I got to know him and was intrigued by him. He was a smooth talker and a good dresser. He indicated to me that if there was anybody we could set up, any kind of businessman, there were all kinds of ways to get money out of such people without getting exposed.

The scheme that he used to extract money from Joe Adamo was simple. I introduced Brown as a manager of one of the piers at Bush Terminal in

Brooklyn. The terminal was a receiving area for all kinds of commodities, and in the receiving of these commodities much salvage and scrap were accumulated – damaged goods and that sort of thing. Brown was in fact not a manager of one of these piers; however, at one point in his life he had access to the place and knew it like he knew the back of his hand. Very brazenly, he took Adamo there, gave him a tour of the place, and asked if he wanted to buy a pile of stuff: "This pile or that pile?" Adamo was very aggressive in business and said, "Sure, I'll buy it all." Now Brown says, "Well you got to make me an offer and simultaneously you've got to put up twenty percent of that offer." Based on the quantity of the material and the estimate of its worth, Adamo came up with his own figure – that there was about $50,000 worth of merchandise he wanted to buy; he put up $10,000 cash. I got $5,000 and Brown got the other $5,000.

Now, of course, Adamo is not going to get his merchandise. My excuse is that I had been introduced to Brown and in turn introduced him to my boss. I can't be blamed for anything. I didn't have anything to do with the deal, and I was $5,000 richer. How did I feel about what I had done; guilty for about all of three seconds. Now, that's got to sound bad, but it's the truth. To me at 21, that $5,000 looked like a lot of money, and at that time it was a lot of money. My wife did not ask me where the money had come from even after I bought a new car and paid a year's worth of mortgage payments. This was an attitude that would continue, even though, later on, she had to know how I was making my money. I always tried to keep my wife and family out of those kinds of activities.

After a year and a half with Adamo, I returned to my father; he had been disturbed that I had gone to work for someone else, but I felt that he really didn't need me. However, when one of his foremen died, I returned to take his place. I was still flush with the success of the con with Brown, and I was ready to set someone else up. I introduced Brown to a guy by the name of Mike (we will call him) Cardi who owned a tire company in Newark. It was a firm that specialized in truck tires, and my father had done a great deal of business with Mike. This did not stop Mike from giving my father a raw deal: refusing to stand behind a warranty when some tires started to have sidewall cracks in them. My father took a different attitude, and as I look back on it now, I was probably trying to find some justification in my own mind to set Mike up for a con. I introduced him to Brown as a person who had access to large quantities of truck tires from a company in Boston and said that Mike could buy at below wholesale prices. Once again I disappeared from the scene of the con; I left it to Brown who walked away with about $20,000. This time, however, Brown didn't want to give me half, only a third. His argument was that all I did was introduce the guy; there is no risk to me. He's coming up with pretty good arguments, so I said okay; it's better to have a little piece than nothing at all.

I was overwhelmed by the thought that it was so simple to get money; it was so easy that by the time that I was 35 I could be a millionaire. That was what I wanted to be. While I made it sound simple, you could not extract money from people quickly. It took Brown a month or a month and a half to get Adamo or Cardi into a position where they were trusting enough to give him some money. It required an investment as well – dinners and broads.

I don't even know the name of the damn committee that was appointed in New Jersey, but it was supposed to look into allegations of price fixing in the garbarge business. Because of the probe, John Serratelli became the righteous union business agent and got out of the 3 percent business; he was concerned strictly with labor. The result was that a refuse collector became the North Jersey shakedown artist in the garbage business. Jim Petro (not his real name) had seen what Serratelli was doing and decided that he was willing to take the chance. Since he didn't have the threat of a strike, he used another weapon. Jim would approach you and say, "Look. your job is about to expire, and the city is advertising in the papers for new bids. You want to get the job again, and you want to get it at a good price." Sure you do; you want to make money – that's the name of the game. "Well, I will lay off the job; I won't bid for the job against you, but it's going to cost you $10,000." Jim would argue that it was not really costing the contractor $10,000 – he would just tack it on to the bid; instead of $100,000 a year, you get $110,000 and the $10,000 goes to Jim Petro. For this money Petro would even enter a complementary high bid. To guarantee that no other contractor would submit a low bid, Petro would threaten to low-bid their jobs. Jim told me that in one year he made about $150,000 to $200,000 from contractors. He was getting fat.

The heat finally died off and the investigation folded. There was a lot of gripes by the municipalities and a great deal of innuendo but no hard facts or evidence. The contractors were angry with Jim Petro whose "favors" were even more expensive than those provided by John Serratelli. They went to Serratelli, who was aware of Petro's activities, and complained. Johnny brought Petro in and told him that he was going back into the "protection" business. Petro didn't like it, and it was at this point I learned who gave Johnny his strength. It was a <u>mafioso</u> by the name of Jerry Catena.* Catena sent an emissary to explain the "facts of life and death" to Petro, who became a very nice passive and low-key contractor; Serratelli was back in business for 3 percent. He went so far as to form a contractor's association known as the New Jersey Municipal Contractor's Association. Johnny was hired by the association as a labor consultant. The presidency of the association rotated, and my father took his turn at the head. Peace and prosperity had returned to the garbage business.

---

* Gerardo Catena was a ranking member and, at one time, acting boss of the Genovese family. During the 1970s he spent five years in prison for contempt – refusing to answer the questions of a New Jersey investigative committee despite a grant of immunity. As they say in organized crime circles, "a stand-up guy."

As time went on the workers became more educated and more concerned about unionism, and Serratelli actually had to create contracts for his members. At meetings with the contractor's association, he told them that they were going to have to pay what was in the contracts. The contractors were not too concerned – they just passed the cost on to the municipality with the legitimate claim that labor costs had gone up. Serratelli also organized the people who owned the dumps where the garbage was disposed of. They were a key element in the refuse business. You could get all the work in the world, but if you don't have a place to take the garbage, you might as well go out of business. One of the requirements of a municipality is that you produce evidence that if awarded the contract you have a legitimate place to dump during the term of the contract. Now, if you crossed Serratelli by bidding low on protected jobs, you would be denied a permit to dump. There was no way in hell that the dump owner is going to give you that permit unless he got a green light from Serratelli. The dump owner has the same motive as the contractors – his rates, and thus his profits, increased. That is the theory of the whole god-damn organized crime: everybody eats and there is peace.

ORGANIZING A REFUSE ASSOCIATION

The problem was that there was no room for expansion. Competitiveness, free enterprise, was taken out of the situation. I could see no way to grow except in one little area, commercial and industrial refuse collection. Instead of doing business with a municipality, a contractor would do business with a commercial outlet, factory, or industrial plant. This was one area that had not been touched by Serratelli, so I said to myself, "You don't argue with success; I'll do the same thing with this end of the business that Serratelli is doing with the municipalities."

I formed an association and sold memberships to private carters. These were more often than not two- and three-truck family operations. The father drives one truck, his brother or son drives the other, and the brother-in-law drives a third truck. It was a highly competitive business, a lot of price gouging. I called a meeting of my membership, and I did not have too much difficulty at all convincing them that there was a lot of money to be made if we stuck together. The comments that I used to make went something like this: "Look what the big boys are doing" – meaning the big contractors – and what they were doing with the municipalities; "they stick together and get their price; everybody eats." I used to make the contractors hate their customers. "These people are beating you; they are abusing you. You've got to raise your prices, and I will guarantee that you will get your price." My biggest problem was controlling these guys because they all wanted to go out and get rich real fast, and I didn't want any bad publicity.

I set up a system similar to the one that John Serratelli had worked out. You are doing the Walter Kiddie plant, for example, and the contract, like most commercial ones, was verbal; you don't have a contract for a period of time – they were on a month-by-month basis. If you went to Walter Kiddie and told the purchasing agent, or whoever was in charge of purchasing the refuse removal service, that you were increasing your fee from $100 to $150, effective next month, he would go the phone book and begin calling refuse companies to make a price comparison. If he could get someone to come in and do it cheaper, you were out and somebody else was in. Among my membership, which grew rapidly, everyone was obligated to avoid underbidding another member's business. If Walter Kiddie called you up and said he wanted you to come over and give an estimate for removing garbage, the first thing that you would do was to call me. I, in turn, would call the contractor who is doing the job and tell him they are looking for someone else to do his work: "What have you done? Are you trying to get a higher price out of them, or are you messing up the service?" This happened many times; the guy's equipment would break down, and he wasn't living up to the performance of his agreement. If I determined that the guy was just trying to raise his price, the word would go out to stay away from this job; or better yet, give Walter Kiddie a price, but keep it high. If you were trying to get $150 for the account that had been paying $100, one of our members would say, "Yes, I'll do the work. I'll come over and give you a price." The price would be $250, and so $150 looked good to Walter Kiddie.

I acquired almost 700 members and was charging $10 a month for association membership. It took me about a year to build up the association, and it was not easy to deal with these small contractors. While some of them were good businessmen, most were not. They were undereducated "muletype" people who ground out a living by just working their butts into the ground. It was an educational process, and I was not an educated person. But, like my father, who was not educated, I was well-read and could get a point across to other people. I never found anything wrong, whatsoever, with performing blue-collar work myself; I never looked down on anyone who did that kind of work. As a matter of fact, I enjoyed it: you're outside and you're hustling and in shape.

As the administrator of the association, there were expenses, but most of the money went into my pocket. Aside from my salary, there were a lot of extras. Although I never established a fee system like Serratelli's 3 percent, I didn't have to. It came voluntarily. If I could straighten out a territorial dispute, a job dispute, or if could get a higher price for someone, it was an unwritten "law" that "silver would cross my palm." I was making about $1,700 a week, only half of which was being reported to the Internal Revenue people. The rest was tax free. And in the 1950s that was a great deal of money.

VITO: AN ILLUSTRATIVE CASE STUDY

MUSCLED OUT

I had been in business for about three years when I was approached by John Serratelli. "Vito," he said, "we can merge our two things." I was being conned and didn't know it. "Vito, we can have a hell of a thing going. We can control all of the goddamn garbage collection business; I can expand your membership even across the river into New York City." The "kicker" was: "But, we got to have a man on the payroll." So John put Ralph Saludo, (we will call him) a soldier in one of the organized crime families, probably the Genovese family, on the association payroll as my assistant. Saludo had done some heavy favors for some high-echelon mafiosos, probably Jerry Catena, and they owed him a favor. Finding a legitimate no-show job was one way of repaying a favor. Saludo used to come in on Friday for his check, $175, and all week long I didn't see him. Gradually, however, he began to come around more than on Friday for his pay. Slowly, but surely, this guy starts spending more and more time hanging around me and in the association office, picking up bits of the operation. He begins asserting himself, making decisions, and giving responses to contractors who had problems. When I went to Serratelli to complain about Saludo, he just shrugged his shoulders and told me not to worry about it. I was being pushed out in a subtle, slow, and methodical way. I had a feeling, fear, that if I did not just put my tail between my legs and allow myself to be pushed out, they would find another way to get me out.

I had a sit-down with Serratelli; it had to be me or Saludo, and at that point I knew what the answer was going to be before I went into the meeting. We met at Serratelli's union office. We both knew the purpose of the meeting, and I started the conversation: "Look, originally, we were going to merge these two things; your words were that we could have a good organization – we could capture the whole garbage industry in North Jersey and even go across the river into New York City. It hasn't worked out that way. This guy Saludo just keeps gaining and taking control. This has been my baby, and we got to work it out some way. If it means me or him, we got to work it out." Johnny's excuse was that higher people, a term meaning Jerry Catena, had made this decision, and they were willing to compensate me for it. They were willing to pay me for the several years of blood and sweat, the organizational ability that I had displayed. Johnny also made it clear that they intended to supplant me with Saludo.

I got so infuriated that I cut off my nose to spite my face; we parted friends, but I left with no money. If I had been a smarter guy, a more prudent individual, I would have accepted reluctantly – but, nevertheless, accepted what was happening – and would have gotten out with some money in my pocket. Instead, I allowed my pride to get in the way, and said, "screw it." As I was walking out the door, Johnny said, "We've got to have your resignation." I sent it in – resigned. "Muscled out" would be a better description.

ENTER JOE PATERNO, <u>CAPOREGIME</u>

In 1957 I bought a small refuse collection route that was owned by Harry Costenzo (we will call him). Harry worked nights at a brewery, and during the daytime he serviced some accounts on a part-time basis. For whatever reason, he wanted to sell the business. Through this purchase Harry and I developed a friendship. One day he was going to a christening party of some distant relative, and he invited me to go along for a few drinks. At the christening party was a man who Harry had known for many years, Joseph Paterno.* At the time I didn't know who Joseph Paterno was, although I noted that he seemed to be treated well, being catered to and shown a great deal of respect. Harry introduced me to Paterno, and sometime later I found out that he was a member of the <u>mafia</u> and that his father, Anthony Paterno, was a don in the organization. Joe had recently been released from the federal penitentiary in Lewisburg, having served seven years for the possession of the back plate of a $20 bill – counterfeit money. He had received a much longer sentence, 15 to 20 years, because he would not reveal who his confederates were or where the other plate could be located. The story was, and I don't know if it is true, that it cost his father, don Antonio, a small fortune to get his son's sentence reduced. Harry said that Joe had a lot of money and suggested that we could work together.

I met with Joe on several occasions, and we discussed the possibility of his getting involved in the garbage business. I also told him about the Serratelli situation. A smile appeared on his face, and he told that he was sorry that he didn't know me before this happened; if he did, it never would have happened. He knew Jerry Catena very well, and Joe's exact words to me were: "We all could have eaten real good off this thing; but it's too late now and I can't do anything." Paterno could have aided me by asserting his territorial right, his authority in Essex County. He could say, "This thing is happening in Essex, my backyard. I have interests in unions and gambling in this area; I have Shylocking interests here, and I want this." What would have occurred would have probably been a sit-down of some kind – at a table very much like this table, but instead of serving coffee and danish, there would have been wine and cheese or anisette and cookies. The problem would have been resolved.

---

* According to material from the Congressional Record, Joseph Paterno is a <u>capodecima</u> or <u>caporegime</u> in the crime family of the late Carlo Gambino (Meskil, 1973, p, 2). This crime family is reputed to be the biggest in the United States. Articles in <u>the New York Times</u> describe Paterno as "a Gambino lieutenant" (Siegel, 1976, p. 60), "Gambino's manager in New Jersey" (Sullivan, 1972, p. 41), and "the top Mafia figure in New Jersey until he fled to Florida to evade a subpeona by the New Jersey Commission of Investigation" (Waggoner, 1975, p. 84).

As it turned out, Joe and I became partners in a corporation known as the V. Palermo Corporation. Because of Joe's criminal record, he substituted his brother Nicholas as my corporate partner. All business, however, was conducted with Joe, and all decisions were made jointly by Joe and me. I went into business with Paterno because I was impressed with his authority, with who he was, and what he could do. I was also impressed with the fact that he had, or could locate, substantial capital. The garbage business is an expensive one to be in – it is a high capital investment business. Equipment is costly; at the time a garbage packing truck cost about $25,000. Paterno was also someone who had the ability to utilize shortcuts because of his connections with unions. I felt that this was going to be a really great marriage.

To commence the marriage, I picked a little municipality in Essex Country called North Caldwell. The city had advertised for public bidding. North Caldwell is a highly residential little community. For many years they had one or more small contractors servicing the residents on a month-by-month basis. If you were a contractor, you would solicit work directly from a homeowner and charge $1.50 or $2.00 a month to take away the garbage. Because of my association – the contractor who served North Caldwell was a member of my association – the price rose considerably. The elected officials decided that they would set up a competitive situation in which one contractor would bid against the other.

The guy that had North Caldwell on an exclusive basis was Luigi Contento (we will call him) . Because of the gouging, the cost had gone to $3.00 a month. North Caldwell officials advertised for public bids. The lowest bidder would be given an exclusive license for the term of the contract. The contractor would be assured that no competitors would come in and undercut him, and the municipality was assured that for the same period of time in the contract they would not be bothered with persistent raises in rates.

When they advertised for this work, I went to Paterno and told him that Contento was in the association that was now being run by Saludo. "I don't want to get my head knocked off if I go and bid this job and take it away from Contento," I told Paterno. Joe replied, "You ain't got nothing to worry about." And I didn't. I bid it at $2.00 a unit and Contento's bid was $3.50. I was awarded the contract, and there were no problems. That was because Contento was "spoken to." Now in street terms that means that somebody from the Paterno organization went to Contento and told him: "Look, you ate on this job for a long time. Now it's somebody's else's time to eat. Don't worry about it – you will get other work someplace else at another time."

I had a private account (we will call) , the Monteray Diner owned by (we will call them) the Schuman brothers, who also built a second diner. Both were more like restaurants than diners, and both did very well. However, because of their expansion they ran into financial problems and couldn't pay me my bill. At the time I was charging about $150 a month, and I went to Paterno. "Oh shit," he says, "we'll get our money. These people are into me."

I asked what he meant. "I got money with these people." Joe had lent them money on a Shylock basis. Right in front of me he picked up the telephone and called the Monteray Diner: "Let me talk to Larry," one of the Schuman brothers. The girl who answered the phone screened the callers because there were apparently a lot of bill collectors chasing these two guys. She started to give Joe the "he's not in" routine: "Look lady, don't give me that shit. Tell Larry that it's Joey on the phone and I want to talk to him. And I want to him <u>now</u>." Larry got on the phone. "Look Larry, I've got an interest in the company that's taking your garbage. You're five months behind on your bill. I want the money and I want it right away." I got the money.

A few months later Joe says, "I don't think we are getting enough money from the Monteray Diner. You tell them that you're going to raise the price, and whatever your raise it to, I'll make sure you get it. Also include $100 for me off the top, okay?" That meant that whatever I got out of the account, I had to give Joe $100 a month. To cover this expense and to make money for myself, I jumped the price to $550 a month. This is one hell of a jump all at one time; the job was worth only about $225, tops. Schuman calls me and he is screaming: "It's extortion, it's blackmail, I'm going to someone else." Calmly, I told Larry to get whoever he wanted, knowing that there was no way he could get anyone else. I received four or five calls from contractors who were contacted by Schuman. I told them to stay away from the job. Being with Paterno was convincing. Schuman called again. He was adamant in not wanting to pay the new rate, although he was willing to compromise and build up the rate over a period of one year. "No good," I responded, and I let his garbage pile up for three days. The stench was overwhelming, and his calls to contractors were of no use. Finally, he called me again and begged to have the garbage picked up, whatever the cost.

There was similar situations with other accounts. The Walter Kiddie Company in Bloomfield, for example. This was a large outfit. I had the account and I wanted to raise them. They paying me about $250 a month, and I wanted to double that. They also squirmed and hollered and attempted to get other commercial contractors to remove the stuff. No one would touch it. They threatened to start doing their own refuse carting, so I went to Paterno. He laughed and said, "Don't worry about it. Where are they going to dump it? Nobody will let them dump it, so charge what you want." I did. I also never had problems with labor like some other contractors did. Men in the garbage business had a tendency to bounce around from one contractor to another. If a driver worked for you and was getting $115 to $125 a week, and wanted to come to work for me, if has a union card he would demand the same salary. If not, he would go to his union business agent who would intercede for him. That would not happen to me. I would tell Paterno and he would take care of it.

LOAN SHARKING

During the course of our relationship, Paterno suggested that I could make some money in Shylocking. If, in the regular course of business, I came across businessmen who needed money and couldn't get it from other sources, I could steer them to Paterno who would lend them money. He put a string on this arrangement: if I sent a John Doe to him for money, I would be responsible for seeing to it that John Doe paid it back. If not, I would be responsible and would have to pay it back myself. At the same time I received a commission on each loan. As an example, there was this Jewish lawyer (we will call), Kenny Berg. He happened to be a pretty good lawyer, but he also happened to be a lousy gambler. He lost it as quick as he made it – sometimes quicker. I knew Kenny as a business acquaintance who I used in a couple of instances, and he knew I was associated with Paterno: "I've got to have some money, Vito. The bookies are banging on my door and I ain't got no cases that are coming up that I can draw on real quick. Can you do something for me?"

It was a small amount of money – $1,000 was all he wanted to borrow. At this point in time Paterno was brazen enough to negotiate these deals himself; later on he insulated himself by having emissaries handle the negotiations, including myself. The deal was made in an office that Paterno had on the corner of Bloomfield Avenue in Newark. It was called the All-State Construction Company, a home-improvement firm, and the guys he had working for him were legitimate people. There was a backroom, as there is in "these kinds of things" – you know, the stereotype backroom that you read about in books. The loan that Kenny Berg made was $1,000 repayable in 13 weekly installments of $100 a week, which meant a $300 profit for Paterno minus my commission. If you missed a week, if you missed one payment, you still have to come up with $50, and the $50 went against nothing – it was strictly vigorish, a late payment penalty. Joe would tell the recipient of a loan very clearly that the money had to be paid back: "It's got to be paid back like I'm telling you it's got to be paid back, and if it's not paid back I'm going to break your fucking legs." These were his exact words, although he would sometimes substitute heads for legs or say, "I'm going to smash your face in." In the case of Kenny Berg I had to handle it differently; after all, he was a lawyer and did do some criminal work. But, he was a sensitive guy, and I wanted to break the waves for him a little bit. "Look," I said, "Kenny there are going to be some overt threats made here, but it's okay. That's just the way Joe talks."

There was a time when Kenny did fall behind on his payments and also refused to pay the late penalty of $50. Joe tells me he ain't seen Berg in a couple of weeks and he ain't getting any money. I called Kenny and he got indignant: "Don't worry about it, I'll pay, and don't call me up at my house." "Well, Kenny," I replied, "if you can't pay the principal, give him the half-yard. You know you've got to keep your word with these people, don't you understand that?" I couldn't get through to him. "Look," I said, "I'm out of it now, and you know who you have been doing business with. I'm doing this as a favor to you, calling you. There's going to be trouble if you don't take care of it." Kenny's answer ended the conversation: "Fuck 'em. I'll take care of it in my own time." I related the answer to Joe. About two weeks later Berg came storming into my office, indignant, infuriated, and scared to death. He accused me of sending collectors to his house for the money. "I didn't send anybody. I related your message to Paterno. I told you clearly what was going to happen. They came to your house to collect their money. Is it their money? Yes, then pay them and they won't bother you anymore." "Vito, they embarrassed me in front of my wife, they insulted me, they threatened me."* Apparently, Joe had sent two heavies, two muscles, and I knew one of them. We used to call him "Apples"; it was his nickname because he loved apples, obviously. Apples was a bad ass. This was the kind of guy who got a big kick out of hitting, hurting someody. They didn't lay a hand on Kenny, but they sure as hell threatened him with some pretty serious bodily harm. Actually, I think Joe was a little cautious and rather conservative in handling Berg who was, after all, an attorney. Anyhow, Berg came running to me. There was nothing I could do. I was not going to call Paterno and say lay off the guy, because then I was going to have to be hung for the money. I advised Kenny: "I don't care if you got to beg; I don't care if you got to borrow; I don't care if you to steal it; get the fuckin' money and pay the man." In two weeks the loan was paid off in full.

There was another customer (we will call), Neil Banto. Banto was a gambler who blew money faster than he earned it by being a tire salesman. He needed money and I arranged a loan similar to the one I arranged with Berg. Banto, however, ran out on me – disappeared. I tried to find him but couldn't. I had to repay the loan to Paterno, although Banto had left after he was about halfway through paying. I got burned for about $600. I once sent a banker to Paterno, a vice-president of a bank in Montclair, New Jersey. He made a $20,000 loan for some real estate transaction. It was a very businesslike loan and he paid it off. In most instances it was not the street person who I sent to Joe – it was the legitimate business guy, or a borderline business guy, who got into financial trouble and did not have traditional sources or borrowing available to him. You would be amazed at the number of people that there are like that. Out of about 150 persons that I sent to Paterno when he was in the Shylocking business, which would have been in the very late 1950s, he only had to send collectors to a couple of other loans.

---

* Rock (1973) reports that in the lawful business of debt collecting "collectors do not engineer status degradation ceremonies" (p. 8).

Paterno got out of the Shylock business in the early 1960s because new and substantial penalties were approved by Congress and the state legislature. Paterno told me that — he said he was getting out of the money business because it was getting too hot; you could really get hurt. What this meant was that in order to insulate himself, he would give sums of money to trusted people to lend out.

THE BIG CON

In the early 1960s I decided that I was going into the disposal end of the garbage business. Environmental controls were becoming more stringent, and the public was becoming aware of the pollution that getting rid of garbage was causing. The politicians started to enact legislation to control this situation, and landfill laws, which had been on the books for a long time, were now being enforced. A landfill is essentially a garbage dump, except that at the end of each day's work you have to cover the garbage with earth fill; you have to make a cell out of the garbage brought in each day. Upon completion of the landfill, which might have a longevity of anywhere from 1 year to 20 years, the entire area has to be covered with two feet of cover material. There were other things that had to be done: prepare proper drainage, provide ventiliation for the methane gas that the garbage produces as it deteriorates, and apply other engineering techniques. If you did not conform to the rules, you lost your permit to operate the landfill in a given municipality. In all of this I saw an opportunity. I had always been well-read in the technology of refuse collection and disposal, and I was a member of several professional organizations: the American Public Works Association, the Institute for Solid Wastes, and the Association of Mechanical Engineers, although I was obviously not an engineer.

At that point in time, there were really only two acceptable ways to get rid of solid waste: landfill and, the more expensive, incineration. In looking at the situation as it applied to North Jersey, more refuse disposal outlets were needed, and the situation was on its way to being critical. I approached some municipalities on a very informal basis in efforts to acquire the necessary permits to operate a landfill. The responses were totally negative. Because of public animosity, there was no way that I could beg, borrow, steal, or lease a piece of land and get the permits that were necessary to operate a landfill. This left incineration.

If you could convince a group of politicians that you would operate an environmentally clean incinerator facility, you might stand a chance. In researching the environmental law and the pollution control law, I came across a New Jersey statute that allowed a municipality, under home rule, to grant a franchise for a period not to exceed 20 years for the construction and operation of an incinerator facility within the confines of a municipality. All you had to do was find a municipality that would allow you to do this. I started to speak, informally, to municipal officials. I put together a presentation package using engineers. The response was negative until I reached (we will call it) Viceroy. They were desperate for a "ratable," a taxable piece of property, a building that they could assess a tax against. An incinerator is a very expensive building; we were talking about several million dollars. This small town had an astronomically high property tax and a piece of industrial-zoned land perfect for the incinerator. I designed a very attractive presentation and made some "presentations" (bribes), and the officials agreed to issue the permit.

The next step was to get money. I had put some of my own money in the preliminaries and a deposit of $7,500 for the parcel of land. I also discussed this venture with Joe Paterno who thought the idea was great; he could see all kinds of dollar signs, and I felt that he could bring me all the business I needed once the project was completed. In addition, I felt that if anything went wrong, I could rely on his financial and political power.

I formed a corporation (we will call) – the North Jersey Incinerator Authority, Inc. I got some static from the New Jersey attorney general because the word authority designates some kind of governmental agency. However, there were no legal prohibitions against the private use of the term, although since that time this has been corrected by legislation. I established two classifications of stock, class A, voting, and class B, nonvoting. The stock was going to sell for $50 a share in blocks of 100 shares. For a $5,000 investment you would get 95 shares of nonvoting stock and 5 shares of voting stock. For me it would be the reverse. This was legit because I founded the corporation, and I could acquire this type of stock for services that I rendered and would continue to render. Several business associates were approached, legitimate people, and I invited them and their friends to an expensive restaurant for dinner and a presentation of the advantages of investing in the corporation. At first things went poorly, but several dinners and presentations later the money began to roll in.

To set prospective investors at ease, I had them send the check to the office of the attorney for the corporation. In a matter of several months, I raised in actual cash about $125,000, still considerably short of what it was going to take to really put this package together. However, during 1965 and 1966 I was drawing $300 a week in salary as administrator of the Incinerator Authority, Inc. In addition, I had several garbage accounts that I had kept even after deciding to get into the disposal end of the business.

If the project was to reach fruition, however, more money would be needed. At the same time I began to get some static from indignant stockholders: "When are we going to get this show on the road. You know you've had my money tied up for one, two years, and I'm not getting any return. When are we going to start making money?" I called a stockholder's meeting, a dinner meeting – steaks, always the best, it wasn't my money – to discuss a financial commitment from the Small Business Investment Corporation (SBIC), which gets its money from the Small Business Administration, a federal agency. The commitment was for $1.5 million and I had been using it as a way to get the stockholders off my back. However, in order to qualify for the loan, it was necessary to produce the financial records of the corporation for an audit. This I did not want to do — not because of my salary, which was legit, but because of some payments that had been made. There had been payoffs to officials in Viceroy, to officials of the New Jersey Environmental Pollution Control Agency, or whatever it was called, and so on. Most of the stockholders were not aware of these payoffs, which amounted to about $25,000. There were also other questionable items. In an attempt to get officials to issue me a permit, I had taken them to the Playboy Club in New York and other such places. I showed them all a good time and, in plain English, a lot of guys got laid. These payments were covered by checks made out to cash in small amounts, $100 to $300, adding up to about $6,000. These items would be difficult to explain to a legitimate lending organization like the SBIC. It would taint the project and keep them from getting involved.

My reluctance to move for the loan resulted in several stockholders suing for the return of their money. I fought the suit and there was not much to worry about; at that time it took about three years for a civil action to get into court — that's how crowded the calendars were. I felt like discarding the whole project, turning it into one big rip-off — it didn't really take me long to get this feeling. I just figured that this lawsuit would make it impossible to get any more money from any legitimate lending institution. It's one thing if the incinerator were already built, but a lawsuit in the embryo stage just knocks you out of the ballgame.

I raised my salary from $15,000 to $30,000 a year and started to drain off the money. I had my attorney give me some inflated bills for legal services rendered to the corporation. In six months I extracted all of the remaining assets, about $100,000; and for all intents and purposes, the corporation was bankrupt. The stockholders started to use funny terms like fraud, criminal fraud, things like that, but it didn't faze me in the least. They were hollow threats, and no such action was ever commenced. The lawsuit did not even come before the courts until, would you believe, 1972, at which time I was in the Witness Protection Program. The Justice Department did advise me that I would have to defend against the suit, and they even went to the expense of bringing me back to New Jersey, giving me all kinds of security protection. The court session was held in camera, no one was allowed into the courtroom except direct participants, and the courtroom doors were locked with U.S. marshals all over the place. I lost the case, and a judgment was rendered against me. I guess it remains rendered against me, and the stockholders are still trying to collect.*

---

* The Witness Protection Program was provided for in the Organized Crime Control Act of 1970. It authorized the attorney general to provide for the security of witnesses, potential witnesses, and their families in legal

THE UNCERTAINTIES OF LOAN SHARKING

While this was going on, I accepted an "assignment" from Joe Paterno. There was this street guy by the name of Carmine Sassone. Carmine had been given some money by Paterno to lend on the street. Carmine was a trusted street soldier, and Paterno did not want anything to do directly with Shylocking anymore. To insulate himself he would give sums of money to trusted people to loan out. The guy that was lending it would get half of the profit; Joe would get the other half. Carmine went to jail for about 18 months, and he had a couple of his guys handle Paterno's money on the street. When he got out of prison, Carmine found some discrepancies, but be became very ill with cancer. Carmine had married a woman by the name of Katherine – "Kathy the Jew" was her nickname for the obvious reason that she was Jewish. This was a very bad broad. When I say "bad," I mean that she had her own criminal record: abortions and paperhanging – all kinds of stuff.

In any event, Carmine dies and Kathy wants to continue in the Shylock business. She has her husband's book that says who owes how much, but she is experiencing difficulty getting her money. She was using very low-echelon street people who were ripping her off as they would collect the money. At the same time, Paterno was not getting his share of the money. He told me about it in passing; it wasn't something that he told me to do specifically: "See if you can get close to the broad and find out what she is doing with my money before I have to get involved directly." So I worked out an introduction to Kathy and started spending time at her house. She was in dire financial straits, and I helped her refinance the mortgage on her house and gave her some pocket money to carry her over during this period of time. At the same time I was able to get hold of the book and find out what was happening to Joe's money. But this crazy broad falls in love with me; it was a question of being there at the right time and befriending her during a difficult period. Her husband had a wristwatch that had 48 diamonds around the face; it had a retail value of about $20,000. How he acquired it I don't know, although I could guess. Besides the dollar value, the watch also

---

proceedings against any person alleged to have participated in an organized criminal activity. The legislation, which was amended in 1977 (with the passage of the Criminal Code Reform Act), authorizes the attorney general to relocate witnesses and their families, providing transportation and housing, "suitable official documents to enable the person to establish a new identity," and assist the person relocated in obtaining employment. The statute permits the attorney general to refuse to disclose any and all information about the identity of the person relocated, etcetera. However, the statute does require that the attorney general make reasonable efforts to ensure witness compliance in civil cases.

had sentimental value to Kathy. Because of our relationship, she gave the wristwatch to me as a gift.

Now I had done my job, and I was no longer interested in continuing my relationship with Kathy. Being aware of the danger of a "woman scorned," I commenced the breakaway process a little at a time. I concocted some stories about how my wife was getting suspicious, and so on. During this time one of her acquaintances, an auto thief, asked her for permission to store a stolen Cadillac in her garage – he was going to store the car until it cooled off and he could sell it. Somebody, I don't know who, and I tell you it wasn't me, "dropped a dime" – called up anonymously and told the police that this woman had a stolen automobile in her garage. The police came and they checked out the serial number, found out it was stolen, and arrested Kathy. She accused me of "ratting her out" on the basis that I had been trying to get rid of her and this was a quick way to do it. I didn't deny the fact that I wanted to get rid of her, but I denied ratting on her because I hadn't.

In any event, lo and behold I get charged with having stolen the car on her word only. This is a hell of a weak case because it's only her word against mine; there is no corroborating evidence. But, the district attorney figures he's got a case. I am charged and indicted and go to trial. Before a jury in Essex County Superior Court Kathy is placed on the stand, and my lawyer tore her to pieces. She got me off as much as she got me indicted. My lawyer dragged out her criminal background, and she lost all credibility. In addition, it was also brought out that I was her lover and that she was a woman seeking vengeance. The jury was out only about 15 minutes when they brought back a verdict of not guilty. Of course, I refused to give back the watch.

As I noted, the watch was quite expensive, and Kathy demanded that it be returned, threatening dire consequences if it was not. The only trouble that I feared was that my wife would find out about the situation, but this was not the kind of trouble Kathy was offering. Instead, she got a fellow whose last name I never knew, but we called him "Jerry the Jew." Jerry was a tall, young man who had a reputation for serious violent activity: assault, assault with attempt to kill, assault with attempt to maim. Jerry was a very vicious guy with a bad reputation. He called me at home and wanted to set up a meeting, and I said sure, "Sure, we'll meet at Howard Johnson's in Bloomfield, New Jersey." At the restaurant Jerry told me right out in front that he wanted the watch returned to Kathy – or I was going to get my legs broken or worse. I am not a violent person, but I asked him if he knew who he was talking to: "I don't give a crap who you are. I want the watch." I told my menacing companion that he was not going to get it and advised him to take back what he had said – "Because I don't want to see you get hurt." I informed Jerry that he was being disrespectful to the people I am with, and if I take it back to them, there is going to be a lot of trouble. I tried to impress upon him just how important "respect" was to the people I was with. He didn't care.

I called Paterno from the Howard Johnson's and he says, "We'll take care of it." Three days later I get a call from Joe: "Meet me at the Mai Kai." This is a Chinese restaurant on Bloomfield Avenue where Italian street people would meet, and Joe used to go there all the time. I arrived at the Mai Kai and walked into the small back room. Joe was there as well as Jerry. One of Joe's men was outside and another guy was in the room we called the "Count": he was involved in numbers gambling. Jerry was apparently associated with him. The meeting only lasted a few short minutes. I sat down and Joe began: "Look," he said, pointing to me, "Vito has something that was given to him and you want it. You want it for yourself or you want it because somebody asked you to get it for them. Now it ain't going back; it is staying right where it is. Do you understand that? Vito is with me – leave him alone. One more phone call, one more meeting, one more threat, and it's all over for you." Now he is pointing at Jerry. Jerry is not saying a word, but he looks over to the Count and shakes his head up and down in agreement. Thank you, goodbye, it was all over. I never heard another thing about it. As it turned out, I lost the friggin' watch in a crap game about three months later.

THE BIG RIP-OFF

I was at home reading the newspaper when I saw an advertisement for a warehouseman in a nearby community. As a lark, a total lark, I went down and applied for the job. I knew nothing about warehousing, inventory controls, and all that. From a three-minute interview with the warehouse manager, I realized that he knew less about running a warehouse than I did – and I knew nothing. Ben Moss (not his real name) had gotten the job through the efforts of his brother Joe, who was president of the corporation that owned the warehouse. Ben was the epitome of the "Peter principle"; he had been elevated to a position that was far above his capabilities. The firm (we will call), the Neuman Corporation, was listed on the American Stock Exchange, and it manufactured expensive ceramic tiles. It had plants in Boston and Alabama, and the warehouse was going to provide a centralized receiving area from which the finished product would be shipped to distributors throughout the New York-New Jersey metropolitan area. The facility was very large, over 10,000 square feet of floor space, and I ran it completely. I filled the orders as they came in over the phone or off the street. Ben spent the entire day in the front office, doing what I don't know. We had one other employee, Judy, a young girl who Ben had hired to take care of the paper work. Judy and I became very good friends – we are sleeping together and I am promoting her, getting her salary raises. This is all necessary to milk the company for everything that it is worth.

After being there for about two months, and by pure coincidence, who should walk into the showroom but Joe's brother, Nick Paterno. You must remember that Nick, as well as Joe Paterno, had absolutely nothing to do with his time. The guy was totally and completely unemployed except on paper. Because of his brother's affiliations, Nick was listed as a consultant for a major construction company in northern New Jersey. He was drawing $500 or $600 a week for a no-show job. With so much time on his hands he would often go window-shopping or look at new automobiles. Apparently he saw that this warehouse had opened up, that they had a showroom where they displayed their wares, and he came in to look. I bumped into him and took the opportunity to outline my plan for ripping off this company, and he suggested that I talk to Joe about it.

It is an unwritten rule that if you are with these mafia people, and you have done each other favors, you must share some of the fruits of successful activities. Joe said, "If you are going to eat, you don't eat alone." You pay tribute; in return for paying this tribute, you hope that if anything goes wrong, that somehow or someway they will be able to help you. Joe, for example, had heavy connections in the Essex County government; the prosecutor's office was one agency that he had influence with. I learned this rule from Joe: "If you eat alone, you're going to die alone." This, of course, could mean a lot of things. It could mean that you wouldn't have any friends, that no one is going to help you. It could, obviously, also be viewed as a threat. However, if you are involved with somebody that is important in organized crime, that person may have some activity in the geographic area that he is in control of that you do not know anything about.

If you are going to become involved in some additional criminal activity in that same area, you may be doing something detrimental to his interests. For example, let's suppose that I was a professional bank robber and I planned to rob the bank on the corner. Now Paterno may be sponsoring another group of thieves, providing financing and giving his approval, who plan to rip off the savings and loan only two blocks away from here. That will bring heat into the area and will be detrimental to his plans and his investment. A professional, whether or not he is directly in organized crime, will often touch bases with the capo in an area he is planning to work. You do this, and you also let him "wet his beak" – give him a small portion of the proceeds. This is insurance money. If trouble would have come in a big way, with law enforcement authorities, for example, Joe Paterno could help. It might be nothing more than getting your indictment put to the bottom of the pile. Delay is always the friend of the defendant. Joe always said that time was your friend: "People forget, they move away, and," he meant this from a violent point of view, "people could take vacations and never come back."

My plan was really simple. I was the receiver of all goods that entered the warehouse. I received the incoming slips for trailer loads of material. These slips would, in turn, go to the front office where Ben would conceivably check them out and give them to Judy who would make the entries in the inventory control book. Because of my relationship with Judy, she made false entries. Instead of putting down 1,000 boxes of number 235 tile, for example, she would make an entry that there were only 500 boxes of number 235, leaving 500 boxes for me to dispose of privately. If you go to the house that Nick Paterno lived in, you will find his kitchen, his bathroom, part of his game room, and his garage walls lined with Neuman tiles that were stolen from the corporation warehouse. Ceramic tiles are very expensive, and I eventually built up a tremendous inventory of my own: I knew what was the company's and what was "mine," so to speak. The next problem, and it wasn't any problem, was finding an outlet for my inventory. There were countless tile contractors who came into the warehouse to make purchases. They were often big guys who employed a number of people and had a lot of jobs going simultaneously. They would make large purchases of tile. My approach was direct: "Can you use some good colors" – not every color in tile was necessarily popular – "at a reduced cost? You've got to pay me in cash." "Are you kidding, I'll take all you can give me," was the usual reply. Customers were no problem, and these were otherwise legitimate businessmen.

I did so much business with these people in cash that in the basement of my home there were three 20 gallon garbage cans, the regular kind that you use to put out for the garbageman to pick up. Only these garbage cans were stuffed full of cash – so much cash that I had to get in the cans and stomp down on them to make room for more. In addition, I was giving a small portion of this cash flow to my attorney in a trust for me in his name. Theoretically, the money could then not be traced to me. I could hardly put it in the bank; here I am drawing a $300 a week from the incinerator and getting $90 a week from Neuman; they were exploiting me; how can you have a bank account with $50,000 in it?

I was also paying tribute to Paterno, insurance that in the event the bubble burst I would get the benefit of Paterno's connections. I paid him 10 percent of whatever I took in and he accepted my word. He said, "I want ten percent of whatever you take in." I didn't have to furnish him with an accounting; if at the end of the week I gave him $200, that meant that I had taken in $2,000 for myself. He didn't ever question my word; I was beating him and he probably knew it, but as long as he was getting something for doing absolutely nothing, there were no complaints.

At the end of the year, in December, we had to take an inventory of the entire warehouse. Naturally, I helped Judy do the inventory and I felt very safe. At the same time Ben was placing more and more responsibility on my shoulders owing to his inability to run the operation. We were building a big business, and the operation was getting to be too much for me to handle. I told Ben that we had to hire someone to help me. He says, "I've got just the guy, and he's out of work. His name is (we will call him) Jim Benson, and he used to work for me in my little tile business. I'll bring him in to talk with you." Jim was younger than me and as naive and dumb as they come. I even made him an officer in the North Jersey Incinerator Authority, Inc.

VITO: AN ILLUSTRATIVE CASE STUDY

I wasn't about to take Jimmy into my confidence because I didn't know him. One day we got an order, a big order of what in the trade is called bathroom fixtures: soap dishes, toothbrush holders, towel racks, and so on. They came in a box called a five-piece bathroom fixture set. It was in a very popular color, fawn brown, and I went through my usual procedure of shorting the load. All of a sudden I realized that a lot of these boxes were disappearing without benefit of having been written down on a sales ticket. So one day a tile contractor came in whom I had never done any illegitimate business with. I told Jimmy to take care of his order, and I went off into another part of the warehouse and watched very closely. I saw Jimmy fill the order, and I saw him go to the cash register and make out the sales slip. The customer got one copy and the other copy would go into a box under the counter. The slips would eventually go to the front office. After the guy left, I sent Jimmy to get coffee and pulled the slip from the box. I noticed that there were items that the contractor had received but that Jimmy had not written down.

Jimmy came back with the coffee and I sat him down: "Jimmy, you gave that guy 15 boxes of tile that are not on the slip. Did you forget about it, or do you have something going for yourself here?" Well the kid — when I say kid, I'm talking about a married man in his late twenties — broke down and cried. "Yes," he confessed, "I had done business with that guy when I worked for Ben before, and the guy paid me in cash." Much to Jimmy's surprise I said, "If you're going to rip off the company, you're going to do it with me, not alone. I'm taking a little bit, too, Jimmy, but you're not doing anything to cover it up. We are both going to get hurt unless you do what I tell you."

Jimmy thought this was the greatest thing since the invention of toilet paper; I probably increased his take by 50 percent. I insisted that I didn't want to see any new cars being bought; you have got to live exactly like you have been doing. Live within your means I told him. And to help drain off some of the money — or to have an explanation for having it — I told him that we were going on a holiday to Las Vegas. I made all of the arrangements. I took $32,000 in cash with me, and Jimmy took about $5,000; and we went off to Vegas. I started to win a great deal of money, but then you lose perspective of what the money really is. In your mind you get the thought: "Oh hell, I'm not playing with my money. Now I'm playing with the house's money." You even lose the idea of what the value of money is because you are not playing with real money — you play with chips, a piece of plastic. Well, I got so hot at the blackjack table that I wasn't even counting the money any more, not counting the chips. I was just pushing a stack of chips forward, and the dealer would just be matching the height of my chips with chips of the same color. In the matter of about an hour at the Silver Dollar, I won about $16,000 and Jimmy was going wild: "Send it home," he advised, "they will take it all away from you again; don't play with it, wire it home to your wife." This was good advice from a guy who I said was not too bright. I lost complete control of myself: "They can't beat me." But they did, and the

Sands across the street took it away from me in about the same length of time. I came back broke, but I had enjoyed myself immensely.

The bilking continued at an even more hectic pace because the business was booming and the material was really flowing in from the factories. I even got a raise: I was actually making $125 by the time I left the job. Suddenly, disaster; Judy finds out that I am married – not only married but I have kids. Now this was a very straight girl. What she was doing was wrong, but she was doing it for me because she was in love with me. I was unquestionably taking advantage of her, using her. She found out that I was married and was heartbroken. I had told her that I was a widower living with my brother and his wife. One day my wife called and the two got into a conversation: "This is Vito's wife," she said, and that burst the bubble. Now this was disastrous. I didn't know what to expect from Judy. She went into the usual hysterics, and we had a meeting after work. She was still crying, threatening suicide, but at least not threatening to blow the whistle on my operation. I was able to calm her down by telling her that it was my intention to ultimately leave my wife, the usual bullshit guys give women in these situations. She calmed down sufficiently in the next two days and said that it would be best for all concerned if she just left the company and discontinued any further contact with me. Afterward we communicated on a few occasions on a friendly basis. It was initiated by me because I wanted to satisfy myself that she was not going to take vengeance on me.

Judy's leaving presented a big problem for me. I now had nobody to make the false entries, and Ben was taking her place until a replacement could be hired. He advertised in the newspapers and finally hired a young woman (we will call), Laura. Laura was there a few weeks, and I was trying to feel her out, trying to figure out an approach. She was single and I took her to lunch a few times and decided to level with her. I explained the operation and said that there would be money in it for her. She was engaged to be married and wanted to sock some extra money away; the deal was made.

Now they say that truth is stranger than fiction, and this will blow your mind. I got into the habit of taking Laura out a couple of times a week for lunch and sometimes to supper as well. During one of our conversations, she says: "I've had a wish for a long time, a desire." "To do what?" I asked. "Oh, you're going to laugh at me." "No, I'm not going to laugh. Tell me what it is." "I'd love to be a – prostitute." I was taken aback and couldn't tell if she was serious or pulling my leg. There was nothing in her background that would indicate this type of activity. She was about 20, tall, blonde, with a pretty face and a good figure. I told her that a lot of money could be earned in this area if she were really interested. She insisted that she was. I told her that she would have to learn the ropes – the kinkiness of sex that some people might expect. She was quite a willing pupil. After a few days of "education," I decided to call her bluff. I told her that I would set something up, and I did. I told Jimmy and a couple of tile guys – I asked them if they wanted to get laid. It was even easier than finding customers for the stolen tiles.

Laura's first exposure to prostitution was six men on the Neuman showroom couch. I collected the money, 20 bucks a shot, but I never kept any of it, I turned it all over to her. Now this has got to sound ridiculous, but it went against my grain to be a pimp. While this activity allowed me to have great control over her, I did not want this kind of money and gave it all to her. I didn't take any cut. I continued to pimp her on a weekly basis with countless people. What amazed me was the demand for this type of service. It is apparently a way of life for a lot of guys. I never kept a tally, but this broad must have easily made $7,000 for herself during the brief time that I was associated with her.

At the end of the year, inventory time rolls around again. Apparently a large shortage surfaced, and all of a sudden I see strange faces coming into the warehouse from the main office. They are tearing the figures apart, and when they can't find the shortage, they bring in an independent inventory company to make the physical count and check it against the records. For obvious reasons, I am not allowed to participate. Everybody starts asking questions, examining the procedures, and looking at the system that was used, and they find gaping holes in the management of the operation. They probably know that Ben is not a totally competent individual, but the thing is blatant. A guy from the main office is brought in to run the warehouse. He starts imposing rules and regulations on me for running the warehouse. They are not impossible to live with if you are running a legitimate operation. For me it's impossible to work under these conditions – for a lousy $125 a week. At the same time management was suspicious of me. The massive shortages pointed to me, although they could not prove it. One afternoon the manager calls me into the front office and tells me that he is letting me go. He doesn't pull any punches; he tells me out in front that a lot of bullshit has been going on and accuses me of being involved with it. Jimmy is to be fired also. "To be fair," he says, "I am going to give you two weeks pay, but I want you off the property immediately."

I'm pissed off now. I'm hot because not only is the son-of-a-bitch taking away my bread, he is also being arrogant to me. "Look Bob," I say to him, "I'm a card-carrying member of the Teamsters Union (which was a lie). Every goddamn delivery that comes in here comes with teamster drivers. Even though this is not a union shop and the normal rules do not apply, you are firing me without benefit of any cause. You are firing me on the basis that you have a suspicion. If you do this, I'm going to see to it that there's a picket line in front of this joint, because I'm a union member. You ain't gonna get any shipments." He laughed, and I was infuriated. "I am shutting this place down," I shouted to him. "Here's your money," he replied. "Now get out."*

---

* I have discussed this incident with several colleagues. All agreed that were they in a similar situation, they would have been only too glad to leave

I was so hot that when I left the warehouse, I went directly to see Joe Paterno. I told him what had happened. "I'll get you a union card, and you be down at Neuman's at 8:00 in the morning. There'll be three other guys there. Get some placards made up: 'On Strike,' 'Unfair to Labor,' the usual shit. We'll close 'em down." The new morning Jimmy and I, along with three of Paterno's goons, started picketing. Sure as hell, at about 10:00 in the morning a tractor trailer arrived. There ain't no way he is going to cross the picket line: "Hi Vito," he says, "what the hell is going on?" "These bastards fired us. They had no cause, and I'm a teamster card man." "Shit," he responds, "there ain't no way I'm gonna bring this load in." And he goes down to the corner store and calls up his shop, telling them that he is not going to cross the picket line. This went on for a week – the warehouse got no shipments. I thought this was fantastic; here's a nobody like me tying up a massive corporation.

One afternoon Bob comes trotting out and says he wants to talk to me. "We are going to start all kinds of legal actions, the labor relations board, the courts, the whole thing. This is unfair to management. We are not a union shop; we do not want to go through all this expense, and I don't think that you want to go through it either because there may be other revelations." He didn't elaborate on what these revelations might be, but he added: "Can't we compromise this situation?" "I want to be compensated," I replied. I said that I'm not talking about compensation in the form of a reference or some other job – I want to be compensated in the form of dollars. He could have gotten us tossed away anyhow because he was legally in the right. What good would it do to continue to harass the company. The whole picket thing was just my way of blowing off steam, vengeance. "Will another couple of weeks severance pay make you happy until you can find something else?" "A couple of weeks," I answered, "I want a couple of months." We settled on an additional $600 and the picket line was disbanded. Again, it wasn't a matter of money; it was a strange streak of pride.

For a 19-month period they came up with a shortage of $350,000; it looks like they got ripped off by their inventory firm also – I had stolen a lot more than that. I had secreted more than $150,000 in cash in my garbage cans. I had also purchased, through my lawyer, a three-acre parcel of land for $15,000. I built my house with the proceeds of the Neuman rip-off; it cost me $150,000. I also owned two Jaguar automobiles and showered my family with gifts: diamond rings, fur coats, and so on.

Neuman without being prosecuted. After all, Vito had systematically embezzled thousands of dollars from the company, so why the "righteous indignation"? Psychopath or sociopath were the frequent conclusions.

VITO: AN ILLUSTRATIVE CASE STUDY

MAFIA HOUSE

I built my house in (we will call it) Mason, New Jersey, and, although it did not start out that way, it became the most pretentious house in the neighborhood. While it was under construction, the money kept rolling in. So, instead of the asphalt shingle roof that the plans called for, I used ceramic tiles, and this required a change in the structure so that the roof could hold the weight of the tiles. Instead of a wooden exterior, I used stone and stone veneer. I made a connection through Paterno and had a 90-foot hall running the whole length of the house covered with marble. There were solid walnut cabinets, a slate floor in the kitchen, and quarry tiles in the dining room. I put in a sodded lawn — instant lawn, because in the morning there was nothing but topsoil all nicely raked and graded and by afternoon there was a whole brand new lawn of Kentucky blue grass. It cost me $4,000.

The house became known in the neighborhood as the mafioso's house. I learned that the neighbors used that term for the first time from my kids: "They think that we are mafia, daddy." Remember, we rode around in Jaguar automobiles and I kept irregular hours. I was an Italian who was in a business, garbage, known to be mob infiltrated or mob connected. Another thing that tended to lend credence to the mafioso image was Nick Paterno, who often came to visit. Nick drove a big, black Cadillac, and if there is anything to the stereotype of a mafioso-type person, Nick would fall into that category. He dressed like one, and he acted like one. He wore black Italian silk suits and expensive jewelry, diamond pinky rings. He looked like a Mediterranean, an Italian, and he spoke like a street person, not too much culture. I never tried to change people's impressions of me, and certainly no one ever asked me directly if I was in the mafia. If they had, I don't know what I would have answered, but nobody ever did. It is not a question that you ask somebody.*

---

* "For those present, many sources of information become accessible and many carriers (or 'sign-vehicles') become available for conveying this information. If unacquainted with the individual, observers can glean clues from his conduct and appearance which allow them to apply their previous experience with individuals roughly similar to the one before them or, more important, to apply untested stereotypes to him. They can assume from past experience that only individuals of a particular kind are likely to be found in a given social setting. They can rely on what the individual says about himself or on documentary evidence he provides as to who and what he is. If they know, or know of, the individual by virtue of experience prior to the interaction, they can rely on assumptions as to the persistence and generality of psychological traits as a means of predicting his present and future behavior" (Goffman, 1973, p. 1).

An incident occurred that added to the <u>mafia</u> image. This little "Mickey Mouse" community of Mason had a garbage contract with a small refuse firm. He provided rear yard collection: he walked behind your house with his barrel, dumped your barrels into his barrel, and carried his barrel out to the truck. At the expiration of his contract, he wanted to change to a curbside service, meaning that the residents of this club community would have to take their garbage out to the curbline. This did not please the board of directors. Because I had been in the garbage business, these directors came to me for advice. I told them not to worry about it, that I would take care of everything. I also did not like having to take the refuse out to the curbline. The dogs are always knocking it over, and it would make the neighborhood look trashy. I told them I would get it all straightened out.

I called the contractor, who knew of me from the association, and asked him to do me a favor: continue his current service for another year. I told him that at that time I would try to help him shift to a curbside service. I intimated that I was acting as his friend, that the directors would not accept the change he proposed at this time. He was reluctant, but he agreed. "I'll go along with it for another year." A week later he completely reneged; he sent a letter to the directors telling them that effective on a certain date the refuse would have to be put out on the curbline or it would not be serviced. Needless to say, this made me look like a fool.* I had told my neighbors that I would take care of it. We were all socially close: we had backyard gatherings, we went to each other's homes, and we went out socially. One afternoon a neighbor from across the street came over and told me that the board had received this letter from the contractor, and they were going to have a meeting — would I attend and was there anything I could do about it?†

---

* "Given the fact that the individual effectively projects a definition of the situation when he enters the presence of others, we can assume that events may occur within the interaction which contradict, discredit, or otherwise throw doubt upon this projection. When these disruptive events occur, the interaction itself may come to a confused and embarrassed halt. Some of the assumptions upon which the responses of the participants had been predicated become untenable, and the participants find themselves lodged in interaction for which the situation has been wrongly defined and is now no longer defined. At such moments the individual whose presentation had been discredited may feel ashamed while others present may feel hostile, and all the participants may come to feel ill at ease, nonplussed, out of countenance, embarrassed, experiencing the kind of anomy that is generated when the minute social system of face-to-face interaction breaks down" (Goffman, 1973, p. 12).

†"An individual who implicitly signifies that he has certain social characteristics ought in fact to be what he claims he is." He exerts a "moral demand" that requires fulfillment (Goffman, 1973, p. 13).

It was a matter of pride: this was going to be straightened out one way or another. At that instant, in front of my neighbor, I picked up the telephone and called the contractor. In no uncertain terms I told him that I was holding him to his word; there would be very serious repercussions: "I will personally see to it that not only will you not have any work in Mason, you won't have any work – period."

On the effective date that the householders were supposed to put their garbage out on the curbline, I told the board of directors that it would not be necessary. There had merely been a "misunderstanding." And as sure as God made little red apples, the contractor came around on his regularly scheduled day and went behind each and every household to pick up the refuse. He also entered into another contract for continued rear-yard service. He apparently believed me when I threatened him over the phone. He knew of my former contractor's association and my connection to Paterno; whichever it was, he was in no position to test me. I saw him on a couple of occasions after that, and he was always quite pleasant to the point of being apologetic.*

STOCKS, BONDS, AND CHECKS

(During the latter part of the 1960s and early 1970s, there was substantial growth in the securities industry. Record sales resulted in hasty expansion on the part of trading companies. The physical security and controls that should normally accompany such expansion were neglected, as companies rushed to capitalize on the sales boom. The result was inevitable: large-scale thefts of bonds, stocks, and negotiable securities.

Prior to the 1960s, stolen "paper" – checks, stocks, and bonds – was not usually recognized as having any value to most criminals. They were accustomed to dealing with cash, jewels, and other such tangible items. Organized crime figures, however, had ready access to this type of paper. Carmine Lombardozi,† for example, is reputed to have had several securities employees under his control as a result of gambling and Shylock indebtedness. These organized crime figures, however, did not have the necessary expertise to convert the paper into cash. They needed the assistance of experts, the paperman.)

---

* "Insofar as the others act as if the individual had conveyed a particular impression, we may take a functional or pragmatic view and say that the individual has 'effectively' projected a given definition of the situation and 'effectively' fostered the understanding that a given state of affairs obtains" (Goffman, 1973, p. 6).

† Carmine Lombardozi was a caporegime in the Gambino family.

One day Paterno asks if I could convert some stocks and bonds into cash: "See what you can work out and I'll give you a percentage. I'm getting involved with other things and I won't have much time for this activity. You work with my brother Nickie." At this point in time Joe was heavily involved in real estate.* He had formed an association with a legitimate Jewish guy whose first name was Howard, but I can't remember his last name.† This guy had a lot of smarts and knew real estate investment.

I had made a connection with a banker at the Lakewood Trust Company in Lakewood, New Jersey, during the incinerator job. I met him in the bank and we went out to lunch. I asked him, probably in more complex terms than I am using here, what would happen if a loan with stocks or bonds as collateral is not paid back. He responded that the bank would sell the collateral and probably realize a profit; they usually only loan 65 to 75 percent on the face value of a blue chip stock. I asked what kind of trouble he would get in personally for making a number of "bad" loans. He explained that it was like in baseball; a Babe Ruth or Mickey Mantle would strike out so many times, but their overall record is good. It's the same way in the bank. I came right to the point: Would he consider a fee for granting a loan? And, if I recall correctly, he hedged a bit, but the bottom line was that he would.

The plan was very simple. Periodically, I would send persons, besides myself, into the bank with stock certificates and phony identification. He would make loans to these individuals using the stock as collateral to justify the loan. If the loan defaulted, the bank was not going to get hurt. If it just so happened that the stocks were stolen and ultimately turned up on the "hot sheet," the bank was still not going to get hurt because they had insurance to protect them against such fraud. Nobody was going to get hurt, and the

---

* Sullivan (1972) reported that New Jersey officials were investigating real estate transactions in the Hackensack Meadowlands on which a football stadium for the New York Giants was built. It was reported that Joseph Paterno owned 21.4 acres of the sports complex site valued (in 1972) at about $90,000 an acre. Paterno was also identified as being partners with his brother-in-law in two realty concerns that owned another 9.2 acres on the edge of the Meadowlands district slated to be developed for business, recreation, and housing. The report identified Paterno as Carlo Gambino's manager in New Jersey and stated that he is believed to be involved in gambling, loan sharking, and hijacking (p. 41).

† "Howard" is apparently Howard N. Garfinkle who was reputed to be an associate of Meyer Lansky, not a "legitimate Jewish guy." It was reported (Seigel, 1976) that Garfinkle had been indicted for, among other offenses, paying $92,000 in kickbacks for loans from a New Jersey union welfare fund that amounted to an outright embezzlement of more than $1 million.

only one who could go to prison was the guy who went into the bank with the stock certificates and happened to get caught red-handed with it. There was no way to trace the individual who had put up the stock as collateral because he was using phony identification. The banker does not have any obligation beyond the normal identification documents to determine who you are. You come in with a driver's license, Social Security card, credit cards, and the like, and say that you are John Jones and have just moved into the area. You want to establish a relationship with the bank because you are planning to open a business and you need some cash. You provide good collateral.

My deal with the banker was that he got 5 percent of any loan that he granted, and I would get 25 percent. Paterno would be given the balance, which he would have to share with whoever secured and whoever cashed the stock certificates. The first stock certificates that were given to me by Nick Paterno were bearer certificates; if I remember correctly, they were IBM. I went to the banker and told him I wanted to borrow against the stock. For a blue chip you get about 65 percent, considerably less on something more speculative. I walked out with $60,000. The banker was eventually indicted and convicted for his activities.

Everybody was happy; we were all eating well off this thing. However, you reach a saturation point with one bank. You cannot continually go back to the same guy and make these deals on a weekly basis. He can usually absorb only about six deals because they are ultimately going to blow up. There are going to be no repayments; it's going to be defaulted, and eventually the stock is going to turn up on a hot sheet as being stolen. This often took a long time because the security houses were totally and completely lacking any kind of security. You could walk into a broker's office in New York City, and on a clerk's desk would be sitting thousands, sometimes even millions, of dollars worth of stocks that hadn't been recorded. Eventually, there were investigations and some tightening up. Anyway, new banking contacts had to be located.

At the same time I developed a technique for bilking banks with checks. Paterno, Nick, and Joe, because of underworld connections, had access to all kinds of things — from the proceeds of a guy breaking and entering a household to guys who performed bigger operations such as commercial and industrial burglaries. I asked Nick Paterno: "You got these guys who break and enter. Do they ever steal checks?"* "Sure," he says, "all the time. But they throw them away because that's how you get caught." I told him to give me the checks, that I knew a way to cash them. Nick threw up his hands: "That's all bullshit, Vito. You've got to have identification and you've

---

* According to law enforcement officials, Joe Paterno sponsored a burglary ring that specialized in business and industrial firms.

got to show your face." I tell him that's true but to get the checks anyway. "Don't throw them away any more." Besides breaking and entering as a source for checks, there was the United States mails. They had a guy who had expertise in robbing the mails. Mike Mariani (not his real name) had made criminal activities a lifetime career. He also made a lifetime career of getting caught at it. It was my association with Mariani that resulted in my one and only conviction. We'll talk about that later. Anyway, Mike had a long criminal record.

The method that I devised was really quite simple. If I have a check that's written out to you that has been stolen from you either in a burglary or from the mails, to cash that check at the bank I have to have some form of identification. For example, if you write a check out to me, I can take it to the supermarket and possibly cash it if they know me; I can deposit it in my account, and it will clear your bank in three or four days; or I can endorse it on the back and go to your bank where the check is written. There I can say that Howard gave me this check and I want to cash it. The teller will ask for some form of identification, which she will note on the back of the check. When you are dealing with legitimate checks, that's okay; but, when you're dealing with stolen checks, you need a different approach. Since it would normally require a constant flow of new identification, and identifications were getting tighter (photographs on driver's licenses, for example), I worked out something else. I devised a scheme for circumventing the need for identification.

If I have your check and a couple of other checks, I also have your checking account number because it is printed on the bottom of the check. Now suppose I had three other checks besides yours. I go to your bank and ask for a deposit slip: "Gee, I forgot my deposit slip. Could you give me a blank one?" Many times that is not necessary because the banks have deposit slips right on the counter. Now I have a deposit slip, and I put down Howard's name and bank checking account number. I endorse the other three checks over to Howard by signing the appropriate name. I then walk up to a teller with two of those checks and the deposit slip and indicate that I want to make this deposit. I am putting money into your account, and the teller nicely takes the deposit. At the same time the third check that I have, which I am not depositing, which may be for any amount of money, $150, $200, or $300, whatever: "Would you mind cashing this for me?" I never had a single refusal. They would cash it and not ask for any identification for the simple reason that I am making a deposit in Howard's account, and she thinks that I am Howard. I have already deposited $500, $600, or $700, whatever the checks are worth, in your checking account, and I'm only asking her to cash a check in the amount of $300 or $400.

Well, the first few times I tried this personally with legit checks it was 100 percent successful. Of course, it was necessary to size up the tellers and pick the one who would not be prone to ask any questions. Sometimes, of course, the person whose checking account I was using was well-known in the bank. "You're not Howard," or "How is Howard today?" or "Where is Howard?" "Oh, he's my brother-in-law and is on a trip. He asked me to make this deposit for him." Accepted every time, no questions asked. Another technique was to use the drive-up window that some banks have, and this would require a confederate. He would be inside the bank looking busy at one of the counters, and I would drive up to the window. If the teller walked away, if she went to ask the manager or otherwise check the situation out, the confederate would be watching. He would signal, brush his hair back, and that meant to drive away. This happened on a few occasions; once I left $20,000 on the counter.

The flow of stolen checks was astronomical, and I was getting more than I could personally handle. I decided to develop an organization in order to continue pursuing this activity on a larger scale. The organization was nothing more than people who were known to Joe Paterno or people who knew Paterno who knew other people who wanted to make a fast, dishonest buck. Paterno would introduce them to me and I would explain the procedures that were to be followed. I would set it all up and prepare the packages of stolen checks. Paterno introduced me to all kinds of criminals – people who participated in illegal activities as their primary source of income. He would say, "This guy's a street guy," meaning he makes his money illegally. A lot of the time I would get a sympathetic comment: "He's down on hard times, having a bad run of luck, and he needs a favor." The faces were forever changing because I did not want the same people all of the time. This scheme required the services of a guy like Paterno who had all these criminal contacts, even with very low types.

I was with Nick Paterno one day when he said: "Vito, I want you to meet somebody who can do us some good," meaning another source of checks. Nick took me to a house in West Caldwell, New Jersey, and introduced me to a fellow by the name of Mike Mariani. Nick told me that Mike had been in and out of trouble and was essentially a loser; that is a guy who is constantly getting into trouble by being caught at what he was doing. Mike had just gotten out of jail for break and entry; it had been reduced from a felony to a misdemeanor and he did his time in the county penitentiary as opposed to the state prison. I felt that with good guidance and good control I could make money with this guy. Believe it or not, Mike was a family type with six or seven kids and a hell of a nice wife. That's one thing that has always amazed me about the criminal element – they always have nice wives. When I say nice, I mean real ladies, nice looking, but not the flashy, show-girl type.

Mike's thing was essentially break and entry, but on occasion he would participate in more violent activities. He was perfectly capable of picking up a gun and using it in an armed robbery. As a matter of fact, during the course of time that I knew him, he did in fact participate in armed robbery. I had nothing to do with that; the use of a weapon to me is a dumb move, a stupid turnoff. You don't need a weapon, other than a pen, to make lots of illegitimate money. I got to know Mike very well, and he had been throwing away all of the checks that he had taken in a robbery or burglary. Like many other thieves, he did not know how to handle paper. Some of these guys would run out right away and try to pass one or two checks. They would often get caught because the person who had been robbed puts the check on their sheet: "My checks were stolen." Right away the bank is alerted. But, as discussed earlier, there are ways to get rid of these checks profitably, and Mike was a good source of checks.

One night he called me up as I was about to go to bed; it was about 11:00. "Come on down to my house. I've got something to show you." I tried to put it off for the following day, but Mike was insistent. I went to West Caldwell to see why he was all excited. Now Mike was a guy who would discuss criminal activity right in front of his family, in front of his wife and kids. You and I would try to keep this kind of thing away from the kids, but not him. He would talk about stolen goods at the kitchen table with the kids around. When I walked in, I saw an array of mail on his kitchen table. He had just ripped off the post office in Orange, New Jersey. A mail bag was just lying on the platform ready to be shipped out and Mike had lifted it. You would be amazed at the amount of cash that people send through the mail. I mean anywhere from $5 in a birthday card to hundreds of dollars for the payment of some bill. Everybody says not to send cash through the mails, but people do it all the time. In addition to the cash, there were also a great number of checks, and that's what I was interested in. And there were a lot of checks on the table. He was very proud of himself, because when you rob a mail bag, it's like a grab bag – you don't know what's in it until you open it up. It could be anything from third-class advertising to who knows what. This happened to be a good bag, which is why he wanted to show it to me that same night. "Terrific," I told him, "put all the checks aside and we'll try to make some packages out of them with deposit slips and what have you. We'll turn some paper."

Mike also introduced me to some full-fledged criminals – I mean people who devote all of their time and energy to criminal pursuits. One guy was called "Biggie." The reason for his name was the fact that he was very big, naturally, weighing about 300 pounds. Biggie had done eight years in Rahway (State Prison) for armed robbery. He had attempted to rob a messenger making a bank deposit, but he had bungled the job and received something like a 10-to-15 year sentence and did 8 of it. As soon as he got out, he went right back to various sundry criminal activities. Now Biggie was a psycho. There were really some screws loose in his head. He could kill without thinking twice about it; he was prone to violence and loved guns. But Biggie was down on his luck at this time, and Mike suggested we use him to hang some paper.

I would always try to avoid hanging paper directly. I may very well participate in such activities by being the watcher, the guy who would give the signal if something was going wrong, but that was it. I would usually avoid going up to a bank teller and handling the transaction personally. Not because I was afraid, but by doing this you were exposing yourself so often that they are going to nail you. The police and the banks will put together a composite sketch rather quickly. Up until this time I was clean; I had avoided trouble and I wanted to keep it that way. The way to do this was to avoid any direct involvement, to insulate yourself as best as possible.

Mike Mariani had stolen a safe from the Wayne Construction Company in Montclair, New Jersey, and borrowed my pickup truck to bring it home and peel it. I had no qualms about this, because my excuse, if Mike got caught, was: "Sure I lent him the truck. He called and asked to borrow it; I didn't ask him what he was going to use it for, and he didn't say." Inside the safe was about $1,500 in cash, of which I got a piece because he used my truck. However, there were also some checks, in particular, one from the Wayne Construction Company – a $35,000 check from the Glen Ridge Board of Education, almost as good as cash. It was written to the Wayne Construction Company for work that had been done refurbishing one of their school buildings.

Usually you have between three to five business days in which to convert a stolen check before it pops up on a computerized sheet used by banks in a particular area. First, it usually pops up on a hot sheet at the immediate bank that it's drawn on, and then the bank in turn feeds the information out to its branches. From there it may or may not go out to other banks in a broader geographic area, but it takes time, usually three to five working days. I know all this because I made it my business to learn banking procedures. A great deal of information came from a couple of tellers I befriended, two girls, in a bank that I did legitimate business with for my refuse firm – I literally picked their brains. At the same time I went to the public library and took out books on banking procedures, particularly procedures used by bank clearinghouses. I needed to know how long it takes for checks to clear from geographic area to area. Today, with high-speed computers, it takes about two days.

I had this big check from Wayne for $35,000, and a few smaller ones, and I sent Biggie to the National Bank in Caldwell to open up a bank account in the name of the Wayne Construction Company. Biggie, following my instructions, told the bank officer that he expected to be doing a big job in the area and needed a local bank in Caldwell on which to draw his payroll checks and so on. He opened that account with an initial deposit of about $40,000, using the board of education check and a few smaller ones, all duly endorsed. Now the bank is going to kiss your feet: you are opening an account with $40,000, and the main check is almost like cash, a government board of education check. Biggie opens up the account on Monday, and I have until Wednesday, possibly Friday, but I'm taking no chances. When you open up a checking account, they give you starter checks, about half a dozen, on which to draw upon until your checkbook is printed up. I sent Biggie to the bank with a $20,000 check drawn against the account Wayne

Construction Company made out to payroll. With the check was a piece of paper informing the teller that so much of the $20,000 payroll was to be in fifties, so much in twenties, so much in tens, and so on. This is a payroll check; I am paying my employees in cash, not at all unusual in the construction trades. My total payroll is $20,000, and this is the way I want it broken down.

Biggie is prone to violence, and there is always the risk that some cutie-pie teller is going to start asking questions and call somebody else over for consultation. Instead of having the ability to talk his way out of it, Biggie might pull out a gun and drop someone. You do that and there are obviously big problems, especially since Biggie is not the hardest person in the world to describe. I tell Biggie that no matter what happens, you must remain cool. To further assure him, I stand behind him in the bank, right on the same line: "Unless I pat you on the ass, you ain't got nothing to worry about, okay? I'll show you which teller to go to." And I picked out a very young girl. Biggie went up and gave her the check, she punched it into the computer that's hooked up to the bookkeeping department to make sure that there are adequate funds to cover it in the account. Because of the nature of the check for $35,000, it went in as cash. The computer now indicates more than sufficient funds to cover this payroll check. The teller starts to count out the money but runs short of some denominations in her drawer. She leans over to the other teller and asks her to borrow some money from her drawer. The other teller is a sharp woman who must have been there since the bank opened umpteen years ago. "You know you are cashing a big check, let me see it." I get a surge of panic – something's wrong. I can't see Biggie's face, but I feel his huge body in a bit of a tremble: "Oh shit, he's getting excited." I keep watching his hands. "Please don't pull that fuckin' gun" is all that is going through my head. The older teller asks a few questions, normal and routine, and Biggie fields them easily. We walk out with $20,000 never to return. There's no way to draw out any more from that account. By Friday it's going to be all over the world that the check is stolen and the account is a phony. I never read about this caper in the newspapers, but banks don't like to advertise their mistakes – it's bad for their image. We split the $20,000 three ways: I got half, and Biggie and Mike split the other 50 percent. Paterno did not get anything out of this particular job; it wasn't a question of each score being broken down in percentages with Joe getting so much from each one. The tribute was a generalized thing, unless Paterno was directly involved in setting up the situation or had some other direct involvement.

One thing that I found strange was that Paterno kept the stolen checks in his house until I picked them up. This struck me as being quite unusual because Joe was always security conscious. He always felt that he was being watched, and I believe that he was actually paranoid about it. Joe would avoid using the telephone and would never talk about any business what-soever on the phone. "Meet me at the diner," was all he would say, and I would meet him at the Andover Diner on Route 10 in Hanover. There we would go in either his car or mine and ride with the radio turned up loud, just in case there was some kind of listening device planted in the car. If it came down to serious business, we would park the car, take a walk through a park, and converse while walking. Joe would often talk in Italian – he used to say: "Talk in Italian so that nobody will understand." This was absolutely stupid. Don't you think the FBI has people that understand this language? If somebody were monitoring the conversation, they would understand Italian better than we understand Italian.* Despite these precautions though, Joe kept stolen checks in his house.

The problem with the check scheme is that you would saturate an area very quickly, and banks communicate with each other. They soon find out that frauds are being perpetuated in their area. Then you have to move to another area, and this requires contacts with people who are operating, stealing checks, in that area. If you are planning to work Essex County, you want checks from banks in Essex County. It was an amazing thing that no one ever got caught. I got 25 percent, the guy who was doing the work got 50 percent, and Paterno got 25 percent from which he would have to pay for the checks. I would get up in the morning and it would not be at all unusual for me to have 10 or 12 deposits ready to go in 10 or 12 different banks with a bottom line for the day of about $8,500. After I had saturated the six or seven counties in North Jersey, there was no place for me to go unless I wanted to continue to move south or across the river to New York. This I was afraid of doing; the banks in New York were much more sophisticated than those at the time in suburban New Jersey. It's a city thing; they are sharp in New York and you're not going to get away with the same stuff there that you will in the Jersey suburbs. So, the scheme just burned itself out after about a year.

---

* Actually, Vito may be underestimating Paterno's strategy in this instance. Statutes governing electronic eavesdropping (assuming the eavesdropping is legal and could thus be used in court) are quite strict. There must be constant monitoring of the equipment to ensure that whatever is recorded is relevant to the court order and not personal or privileged – e.g., between husband and wife, lawyer and client. Under 1968 federal statutes, two recordings must be made simultaneously. One is continuous and at the end of the order must be sealed and turned over to the court. The second is monitered and must be turned off whenever nonauthorized conversation is being conducted. The monitoring agent must take off his/her headphones and place them in a soundproof box. An agent's falling asleep can result in weeks of recordings being suppressed by the court.

Thus, communicating in Italian would severely limit the number of agents available for monitoring and would make (lawful) eavesdropping very difficult.

THE CAMPISI FAMILY

In the Italian enclave of Vailsburg, in Newark, the Campisis are known as a crime family, but in reality they are a family of criminals. That is, they are not the equivalent of the Gambino or Genovese families, yet they had an organization made up primarily of actual family and some associates that dominated gambling in the Vailsburg area. While at least a few Campisis are reputed to be members of the Genovese or Bruno (Philadelphia) families,* they operated essentially as a separate unit, accepting only a minimum of discipline and leadership from the major families. The Campisis have been referred to as a "renegade crime 'family,' " but this is not quite accurate. What is accurate is that the Campisis were a rather wild and quite violent group, a situation that made them a prime target of federal and state law enforcement agencies – local agencies were notoriously corrupt. The Campisis provided "enforcement services" for the major families, and robbery and murder were added to the repertoire of Campisi activities – more than a hundred robberies and eight known murders.

I met the patriarch of the Campisi family, Anthony Campisi, whose nickname is Nanay, through Nick Paterno.† I was introduced to him in Campisi's home in the Vailsburg section of Newark. The introduction was the result of discussions with Nick relative to securing more checks and stocks for conversion to cash. Nick said he had some "good people" in organized crime circles, meaning that they could be trusted, who were a source for this kind of paper. He wanted me to meet them and work something out. So one day I went with Nick to see Nanay. We went to Campisi's house and Nick made the introduction: "Vito, this is Tony Campisi." Tony responded: "You call me Nanay." And we sat down in Nanay's living room. His wife brought us coffee and cake, and Nick left the room without saying anything and went out into the front yard of the house. This meant that he did not want to hear what was going on; he wanted to avoid direct involvement; this is an insulating factor. In the event of a backfire, somebody gets nailed: "Who was present during the discussion?" "Just Vito Palermo and Nanay

---

* Vito states that he was told that the patriarch of the Campisi family was a member of the Bruno family.

† "One can also build on intermediaries who have relationships with others. By being introduced, given a letter of recommendation or a formal credential, or invited to someone's home for a party, one can widen his network of acquaintanceship. In effect, the exchange of trust already negotiated by one's sponsor becomes surety for entering into relationship with strangers on a deeper level of commitment than otherwise" (Collins, 1975, p. 141).

Campisi." "Wasn't Nick Paterno there also?" "Yes, but he was out on the front lawn; he had nothing to do with the discussion." An insulating factor.

Nanay said that he had connections for stock certificates and checks and that he had learned through Nick that I can get rid of the stuff. "How much can you handle?" "Not a great deal at one time, but enough to make it worth the effort for everyone involved." Okay, I got a shipment coming pretty soon — stocks, good stuff. When I have it, I'll call you." We exchanged phone numbers, and the whole thing took about 15 minutes, with most of the time spent drinking coffee. When we got back in the car, Nick asked, "Are you going to work something out?" I answered that we were and that I would keep him posted.

At this point in time I had already been convicted of a felony and was out on bail pending the appeal process. I was not anxious to get involved with the Campisis; I did not need any trouble at this time. But, there was little or no alternative, unless I wanted to make some dangerous enemies. I doubted whether Joe or Nick Paterno would hurt me physically, but Nick had asked me to work with Nanay. There would be a lot of questions raised if I declined: "How come after all this time you're reneging, you're backing off? Everything that we've done for you, for each other, all the trust, all the faith." The confidence would be gone and maybe, just maybe, Joe might get a bug in his head and say: "This guy is turning, getting cold, turning against us. He's got a lot of information and maybe he's going to say something." And maybe I would get hurt, even whacked out (killed). Again, that would be doubtful, but Joe was capable of it and it is something that stays on your mind. You find yourself boxed in. There is an old expression that there is only one bonafide way out of organized crime — feet first. I was not anxious to test that out with the case of Vito Palermo.

About a week later I got a call from Nanay and we arranged to meet in a diner in Morris Plains, New Jersey. He was with two of his sons and his nephew, Petey White and Petey Black, and the other son I think was Carmine, I'm not sure. We met inside the diner and went outside to Nanay's car. He reached under the seat and produced a brown envelope, which upon opening revealed that it was loaded with blue chip stock. I'm talking about Ford Motor Company, IBM, Xerox — good stuff all in bearer name, not made out to any particular individual. In the right hands, my hands, they were as good as cash. I did not want to take the package without doing some checking. I asked if I could merely take some of the numbers off the certificates, and Nanay offered the whole envelope. "No," I told him, "just pick out some at random and let me write down some of the numbers. I have to check them out with my sources."

I wanted to see if the certificates, the numbers, had turned up on any hot sheet. As it turned out, none had. In other words, the brokerage house from which these stocks were lifted did not even realize that they were missing. What I do with the numbers is merely walk into the bank and ask to see the hot sheet. It's a document that is readily available, but it would probably raise some curiosity or even questions in a bank – unless you knew the bank official. But, I was doing business, legitimate and illegitimate, with this guy, so there were no problems. He was the president of a savings and loan association and was eventually found guilty of misappropriating savings account money.

Several weeks actually passed from the first time I met with the Campisis in the diner, checked out the numbers, and finally accepted some of the certificates. I was in no hurry to do business; I was still jumpy. I found out that the Campisis were desperate for money. Nanay owed considerable sums to Paterno, money that he used to finance his bookmaking operation in Vailsburg. The operation had been hit very hard with a couple of big winners, and they were hurting. In addition, they were somewhat outcasts because they were dealing with drugs, an activity that, at the time, was a total "no no" to Paterno and Gambino. Of course, this had nothing to do with morality – drugs being "dirty" and all that crap – but was based on the heat that dealing in drugs would cause. Federal agents would climb all over your operation if you also dealt drugs on a big level. Nanay even asked me if I knew of any place or places that had substantial sums of money, a place they could set up for a robbery. Nanay's brother, the one who was dealing drugs, was apparently keeping the biggest portion of that income for himself and was just throwing some crumbs to his brothers and his nephews. "Vito, if you know of any place that you can set up where they have a lot of money, a supermarket, a bank, a warehouse, anything; we got to get some money." Armed robbery was not in my line of work, but I told Nanay that I would keep my eyes open. Nanay was desperate; the Campisis had legal problems, and these were mounting; and the lawyers were prostitutes and opportunists. They get a client who is known to be in organized crime and they charge whatever the traffic will bear. The lawyers that the Campisis had engaged were renowned in legal circles – renowned for the fees that they charged. This does not mean that they were necessarily all that talented in the law. However, they knew how to work the courthouse, to get delays, and this is important. Delay, as I mentioned earlier, is the friend of the defendant. The prosecution begins to have trouble with witnesses; in one case, during a period of delay, the Campisis killed a witness. Petey Black and Ira Pecznick* had been picked up for an armed robbery, and they

---

* Ira Pecznick is probably the most controversial case in the history of the Witness Protection Program. A vicious executioner for the Campisis, he turned against them, received a pardon, and became a client of the program. He is currently at large with a new (government-produced) identity (see Aronson, 1978).

The murder that Vito is referring to received a great deal of media coverage in New Jersey. The victim, Gerald Mass, was a 43-year-old payroll messenger who had been robbed by the Campisis in 1969. When he became a witness against them, Pecznick and several Campisis kidnapped him on July 1, 1971, strangled and shot him and buried his body in some woods.

subsequently did away with the only witness. They were also trying to buy all kinds of time for themselves, to delay their case, and that gets expensive. The Campisis were looking for money from any source.

I began working with the Campisis on the check scam. The fact that Nick Paterno had made the introduction and was present during the initial conversation meant that in the future if any disputes arose between Nanay and myself, Paterno would settle them. Of course he would also get a tribute from any of our deals. I took some of Nanay's checks and converted them into cash in a few days; all totaled it was about $13,000 after expenses. Nick got $1,300 and Nanay gave his half to Paterno to satisfy his debt. I did business with Nanay for several months. In one scheme, I asked him if he knew of any store owners, a guy who might own an independent supermarket or bar — something that had a good cash flow with a sizable checking account balance. He said he knew someone and that the guy was a stand up, meaning we did not have to worry about him. The scam was to have the store owner go away on a legitimate vacation for a few weeks. While he is gone, we "steal" his checkbook and write checks against his account. We would draw everything off except a few thousand. The store owner now returns and "discovers" that his checkbook is gone — "stolen." He checks with the bank and learns that his balance is down considerably. Pointing out that he did not have these funds drawn out, the bank checks out his signature — forgery. While the forgery is not really hard to spot, banks are so busy, especially with larger accounts where a lot of checks are written, that they seldom look carefully at the signature. The end result is that we clean out about $60,000. Expenses, money for the people who pass the checks, are about $15,000. Nanay gets $15,000, the store owner gets $15,000, and I get $15,000. The $15,000 for the store owner is clear profit — untaxed. Since the bank was negligent by cashing forged checks on his account, the money is replaced by the insurance company. I gave Nick $1,500, and I don't know what Nanay coughed up.

Another scam I worked with Nanay was bank money orders. I found a small bank in Roseland, New Jersey, that was issuing money orders without benefit of a check-writer; they would merely type in the amount. I bought about $60 worth of money orders in very small amounts, 12 in all. Through a process — I won't bore you with the details — I changed the amounts, "kited" them to sizable amounts. I then gave them to Nanay* who would send them to a contact in Las Vegas where they were converted into cash. The scheme eventually ended when the bank realized what was happening and converted to a check-writer.

---

* The Campisis were prosecuted for murder, robbery, and racketeering. As a result of a plea bargain agreement, they pleaded guilty to lesser charges and received relatively lenient sentences.

ORGANIZED CRIME: RULES, ROLES, AND ORGANIZATION

Italians from certain sections of Italy, the south, Naples and Sicily, are very clannish and vengeful. They also believe that if you see something wrong, you have proof of crimes, you totally and completely keep your mouth shut. Among these Italians is a very small segment who devote their energies and their intellect to criminal activities. They have certain hard-and-fast rules that, if you want to become part of that group, you have to embrace and accept. Joe Paterno only had to tell me once: "Anything you hear, anything you see, stays with you, in your head. You don't talk about it. You don't ask questions. What I tell you is enough for you to know, enough for you to carry out the instructions that I give you." It's a blind kind of a belief, and there's no doubt that it takes a certain kind of individual to be able to accept that kind of teaching or philosophy.

It's also a macho thing as well; you are one of the boys and there is respect associated with that. You are looked upon as being a stand-up individual, which in street terms means a person who can take excessive punishment, deserved or otherwise, and still keep your mouth shut, not reveal who may have participated with you in any given kind of activity. You protect that other individual or individuals, and in return you expect him to protect you. At one point in my life I was completely prepared to accept death as opposed to ratting out or turning in somebody who I might have been associated with in any kind of criminal activity. It's something that you have to become exposed to in order to really understand. There is no set of bylaws, nothing written down on a piece of paper. You learn these rules from others; it's a word-of-mouth kind of thing. I learned them from Paterno.* You accept them or you do not belong; you will not be allowed into the inner circle, and it is recognized immediately whether you want to accept this because you show it. It reflects in your attitude, this kind of thinking.

I never met anyone who was introduced to someone as a gli amici degli amici, a bona fide member of the organization, who was not Italian or who did not have an Italian-sounding name. In my case, it would have been sufficient for Paterno to say, "Vito is with me."† These words were enough for any others to accept me. If one is not an Italian, or at least part Italian,

---

*Secret societies promote rules of secrecy by the oath and the threat of punishment. "More interesting," Simmel (1950) notes, "is a technique that is sometimes encountered, namely the systematic instruction of the novice in the act of silence" (p. 371).

† According to the "De Cavalcante Tapes," members of organized crime are referred to as being "with us." Being "with me" apparently refers to a trusted nonmember under the aegis of a patron.

there is less trust. Italian organized crime elements are very clannish; they put a great emphasis on the feeling that this is something inborn; it's the macho thing again. The Italian is a stand-up guy, a quality they apparently do not believe exists in other ethnic groups. I don't want to create the impression that every Italian person is a <u>mafioso</u> or a criminal – my own family disproves that.

My meaning of <u>mafia</u> is that there are in fact a group of people who are tightly knit by virtue of ethnic and family ties who participate in all forms of criminal activity on a highly organized basis. There is an interrelationship between one group of organized criminals in one city, or in one state, and another group, or groups, of organized criminals in another city or in another state. I call this <u>mafia</u>; this is the term that Joe Paterno used – he considered himself a member of the <u>mafia</u>. I remember once that Joe and I were sitting at a counter in a luncheonette in Newark; we had both come from a barbershop and we went into this coffee shop. This would have been around 1958. We were talking about an individual who we both knew who had just gotten caught in a criminal activity involving gambling. Joe said to me that if he had been a member of the <u>mafia</u>, it would not have happened. On another occasion, Albert Anastasia was pointed out to me by Joe Paterno; it was at the funeral of don Antonio, Joe's father. Joe, who was taller than me, put his arm around me and I looked up at him: "See that guy over there," he asked, "do you know who that is?" "No," I responded. "Albert Anastasia." Now it sounds sick, but I am telling you that this was the epitome of respect – Albert Anastasia had come to don Antonio's funeral. When Anastasia was knocked off, both Joe and Nick Paterno, on at least two separate occasions, commented that the <u>mafia</u> can live without him: he was a mad dog; he was a killer;* he made a lot of noise and brought bad publicity to the <u>mafia</u>.

I noticed the word <u>mafia</u> disappearing from the criminal vocabulary by the mid-1960s, when it was called the organization or the syndicate by Paterno and others. The only thing that comes to mind as the reason for this

---

* Albert Anastasia was widely-feared. During the 1930s and 1940s he was the patron of a unit of Jewish and Italian criminals in Brooklyn dubbed <u>Murder, Inc.</u> by the press. As the name implies, this group specialized in "contract" murder; contracts were passed through Anastasia by organized crime groups throughout the country. It was members of this unit who were responsible for the murder of Dutch Schultz (Charles, "Charlie the Bug," Workman, one of the executioners, was on parole, to my unit in New York). Anastasia reputedly enjoyed the title: "The Executioner." Albert's brother, "Tough Tony" Anastasio (different spelling), headed the International Longshoremens Association (ILA) on the Brooklyn waterfront. The recently convicted ILA leader Anthony Scotto, is married to Tony's daughter. For an account of <u>Murder, Inc.</u>, primarily through the revelations of one of its members, Abe ("Kid Twist") Reles, see Turkus and Feder, 1951.

is the heat brought on by congressional investigations into organized crime. Joseph Valachi referred primarily to La Cosa Nostra, which he loosely defined as "our thing" or "our organization." I had never heard that term before it was used by Valachi in reference to organized crime. Afterward, however, low-level people began to use it, but Paterno and other high-level organization people never used the term in front of me.

Don Antonio

Don Antonio, Joe's father, was highly respected. When I say highly respected, I'm talking about in the criminal community. It's something that you have to be exposed to in order to understand, and I don't know whether I have the vocabulary and ability to convey what this means. But, I'll give you a little example. In the front office of Joe's business headquarters on Bloomfield Avenue in Newark, there were always three or four "wise guys," hoods, hanging around, including myself. When Joe's father used to come into the office, we would all rise, get off our chairs. You would approach don Antonio, you would extend your hand to him, and in a greeting you would embrace him, if he allowed you to. If you were not in his good graces, or if you were not friendly, you weren't an acquaintance or associate, it was considered an absolute "no no" to touch this man – like he was a god of some nature.*

To show you what kind of god he was in the criminal community, when he died, this was nearing the end of the mass type of criminal funeral you would see in the movies or read about in books, although there was still a semblance of an earlier era, people came from all over to this man's funeral. I'm talking about from the lowest scum in the gutter to elected and appointed officials. There were judges, a congressman, lawyers, and people such as Anastasia and Frank Costello† – they were all there. The FBI was

---

* The son of a New York crime family boss describes a similar situation (Brenner, 1981):

My father would light a cigarette and five people would jump to push the ashtray close to him. At a dinner, people would wait to speak until he spoke to them. If he put down his fork, you stopped eating, even if you weren't finished. My father was god to everybody. (P. 18)

†Frank Costello, a Calabrian whose real name was Francesco Castiglia, was a corrupter whose adopted Irish name was no handicap in a city dominated by Irish politicians. Wiretaps made public reveal that he had the power to engineer the appointment of judges, and he is reputed to have been a major force behind the election of Mayor William O'Dwyer. Costello was

parked across the street taking pictures of the license plates and the people that were coming in and out of the funeral home. I took my brother with me to the funeral. "Come on, we'll take a ride," I said to him. He really didn't know what I was involved in and he spots the FBI guys: "What are they doing?" I tell him that this guy was a racketeer, and my brother gets all excited because he is afraid they would take his picture and license plate number — my brother is a very legitimate person.

I always called Joe's father don Antonio. Once again, this relates to something that I don't know if I can explain. I was being groomed for membership in the organization; I had a closer relationship with the old man than an average street guy — I was partners with his son. Street soldiers in Paterno's organization would call him mister, but I had a closer relationship, one that meant that I was able to call him don Antonio. This term would only be used by people associated with criminal activities; legitimate people would not call him "don." Joe told me that his father had come from Sicily and had risen in the criminal ranks of Newark, taking charge of rackets and other things. However, it was the war years that put his father ahead of other racketeers. He made all kinds of money during the war years, especially in the black market.*

(Vito was present when Paterno requested help from his patron, Carlo Gambino.)

Joe Paterno had requested help from the "old man," Carlo Gambino. Paterno was apparently in conflict with a member of the Bonanno family who was involved in Shylocking in Paterno's area. The guy was taking away customers from Joe, and Paterno had had someone from his organization talk to this guy, but to no avail. Joe could not take direct action against this guy because he belonged to the Bonanno family, so he turned to Gambino.

---

closely allied with Albert Anastasia. In 1957 there was an attempt on his life, followed by the murder of Anastasia. The aborted "crime conference" in Apalachin, New York, in 1957, raided by the state police, was reportedly convened to discuss these events, which, according to Valachi (Maas, 1968) were engineered by Vito Genovese.

* Ralph Salerno, in a lecture at the North Carolina Justice Academy, May 1979, stated that he had asked Joe Valachi what was the most lucrative enterprise he was inolved in — loan sharking, drugs? "The black market during the war" was the response.

A top-level meeting was arranged. It took place in the St. Regis Hotel in New York City in, I believe, 1959. Paterno, Charlie Apple, and I went up to the twelfth floor to see the old man. Incidentally, the term old man would never be used except among ourselves; there is no way you could call Gambino, to his face, old man. That was like calling the pope a whore; it was a matter of respect. I always addressed him as don Carlo; that is the way I was told to address him by Paterno. Joe knocked on one of the doors, which was opened by an individual I did not know, apparently an associate of Gambino. After the social amenities and some drinks, there was a knock at the door. It was Joe Bonanno and an associate. There was much smiling, handshakes, and embraces; the embrace included a kiss on the cheek. This is not necessarily a sign of affection that is displayed just among criminal elements that belong in the mafia, it is a social amenity that is often displayed by everyday Italian people.

Gambino's associate, Bonanno's associate, Charlie Apple, and I were all introduced by our first names. Joe turned to me. "Vitone," he always called me by my Italian name, "I want you to meet don Giuseppe." (Vito already knew Gambino.) Bonanno was a very striking man, a handsome, well-built guy. We shook hands and this was repeated for Charlie Apple. Paterno and Gambino sat on a little couch and Bonanno sat down in a chair on the other side of a coffee table. The rest of us busied ourselves doing nothing. We did not socialize; we did not form a separate social group and start talking about the weather or about sports. We acknowledged each other's presence, but that was all; we each did our own thing. My thing was to look out a window while drinking a glass of wine.*

There were no harsh words exchanged during the meeting, but there were firm words. You would have to be an idiot not to know that this was a serious matter. Gambino made a threat, but it was not to Bonanno's person; it was to an associate, a member of his family.† The typical approach is as follows: "Your brother-in-law, your cousin, or your associate is bothering me, giving me some problems. I already spoke to him, and he seems to have

---

* Goffman (1974) refers to this as "out-of-frame activity," whereby certain persons will be disattended – "present in a relevant way but treated as though not present" (p. 207).

† The Bonanno family is reputedly the smallest of the five crime families in New York City. Joseph Bonanno, born in Castellammarese del Golfo, was aligned with Salvatore Maranzano in the Castellammarese War. His underboss was Carmine Galente whose murder was referred to in the last chapter. For an in-depth journalistic look at Bonanno and his family, see Talese (1971). In 1981, Bonanno was convicted of conspiracy to interfere with a grand jury investigation. He was 76 years old.

a very bad attitude about this. Look, you're closer to him than me; you tell him to get off my back, or get out of my face, or else I'm going to have to take other means." The "or else" in this instance refers to violence. The man has already been advised; he has already been spoken to – in this case, by one of Paterno's lieutenants who warned him to stay away: "You got no business putting money on the street in this area, or dealing with the particular individual or company." That came from a very high source. You, being in the organization, have got to respect the weight that it carries. Now you have been given one respectful but direct warning and have chosen to disregard it. Bonanno said: "I'll take care of it. You won't have any more problems." And I guess he did. I never heard any more about it.

(Vito notes that Paterno was his patron, just as Gambino was Paterno's patron.)

You pay tribute, a fee, sometimes predetermined, to participate in criminal activities in a given geographic area. This tribute is paid to the person or persons who are in charge of that particular area. Now in my situation, Joe Paterno was the person in charge of the geographic area that I worked and lived in. He was in charge from the point of view that he would be aware of many of the criminal activities that occurred in the area. It does not mean that the person in charge has given permission for the activity or is getting tribute from it. There are a lot of things that go on in an area that the other criminal elements do not know about until such time as it hits the papers.

However, when you are a person like myself who knows that there are certain organized criminal activities being conducted in your area, then you have the obligation to tell the person in charge that you are going to get involved in something; for lack of better words, to get his "permission" and "protection" in the event that something goes wrong. You pay the tribute for that protection. You pay for the privilege to do business just like you buy a McDonald's franchise and are guaranteed an area. The area under the domination of someone like Paterno is determined by virtue of family territorial rights. Carlo Gambino, for example, stakes a claim for certain geographic areas in which he declares that anything going on in the area belongs to him: all numbers sold – all organized betting of any nature, football, horseracing, crap games, whatever it might be – are organized and dominated by Gambino. Like any other business organization, he needs to delegate authority to have these functions operate efficiently.

Paterno, for example, is in charge of the greater Newark, New Jersey, area. He would get a piece of all the criminal action going on in that area, and it is his responsibility to make sure that Gambino was being protected and was getting his proper share of the revenue being generated. I was paying tribute, and was tantamount to being a free-lance franchisee; that's the way I would look at it. I had the right to do my thing within the geographic area where all criminal activities of any nature were being overseen by Joe Paterno; he would grant me that right. Now you pay a franchise fee, this tribute, for several reasons. First, it is a matter of respect. I don't know how to explain it to you, because I am not sure that I understand it myself. Let me give you an example of what is meant by respect. There were these two guys, independent bookmakers. Both were Italian and involved with various criminal elements, and both had gotten into trouble with the law. One of these guys had an office in Kearny, New Jersey, which was essentially a legitimate front for his other activity, a construction firm. His office was very plush in an area that was really run down and depressed. One day I went to his office to discuss a piece of property that he owned in an area that he said he could get municipal permission to utilize as a landfill, as a dump. I looked upon it as a situation in which I might be able to develop it into a usable disposal site and sell usage to small independent contractors who needed a place to get rid of their garbage.

I went to his office and the conversation moved its way toward criminal activity, those things that he was involved in. His words to me were: "I hear you're connected with some people up on the avenue," meaning Bloomfield Avenue in Newark, which is where Paterno's headquarters were. I said, "Yes, I know some people up there." He asked, "Who?" I answered, "The person who runs the avenue," not using Paterno's name unnecessarily – another rule. "Who, Paterno?" he asked leaning back in his chair and laughing. "He's shit. He can't do nothing."

Upon hearing what he said about Paterno, I had an obligation to tell Joe what this individual said for two reasons: the first is that if I did not tell Joe, and he learned from another source, he would be very angry. He would say to me: "Vitone, this guy said this about me to you, and you didn't tell me about it. You let me continue doing business with this son-of-a-bitch." Second, and very selfishly, I had another problem. What if this was all a test: Paterno is suspicious, even paranoid. Maybe this guy did this to see how I would react: would I report it to Joe? Late that afternoon I went to Joe specifically to tell him about this conversation. This was one of the few times that I ever saw him get infuriated, lose his temper. Joe was always supercool, but now his face reddened. Charlie Apple was there and Joe said to him (and these are his exact words): "Charlie, I want you to take Vitone in the car with you right now. I want you to go down to see – – – "(the guy's name escapes me). "I want you to walk in and I want you to smack him in the mouth and tell him who sent you."

The reason for demanding that I be there was so that Paterno would not lose any face with me – to show that he is the boss. Well, Charlie and I jumped into the car and went down to Kearny, which is quite near Paterno's office. We walked right in, passed his secretary, and went into his inner office. The guy was sitting in his nice big leather chair behind his desk tending to some paperwork. He looked up and started to stand. Charlie just reached across the desk and hit him with his fist straight in the mouth, splattering his lips and sending him backward over his chair: "This is from Giuseppe," Charlie shouted, and we turned and walked out. When we got back to Joe, Charlie said: "It's taken care of." I never heard any more about the matter. Incidentally, this guy and his partner were indicted for coercion and bookmaking, and I think they did some time.

(A key element in organized crime is monopoly: the ability to control or otherwise regulate competition.)

If someone comes into an area and begins to operate without permission, he is liable to hurt someone that is already in the game. At a minimum, he can create waves, attract law enforcement attention. That is one of the reasons you pay tribute, to ensure protection from the law and from unregulated competition. If you come into an area and start hanging some paper, you are adding to the heat in the area. If I got a nice smooth operation, I don't want anyone interfering with it. If I find out about you, who you are and what you're doing, I go to Paterno. "Do you know this guy, Joe? Do you know where he is from? Who is he connected with?" Joe is going to find out all about this person; this is easy. You are making contracts, you are seeing people, and you are not that hard to find. And someone from the Paterno organization is going to visit you. He will say: "Look, we got this thing tied up over here. We're running a nice quiet little operation, so do yourself a favor, and do us a favor: cut it out and go somewhere." Now if you are smart – if you have street smarts – you will have known who Paterno is when his name is mentioned. You are going to say: "I'm sorry. I apologize. I didn't realize it." Then you close up shop. If you are not smart, if you persist, the next step, the second step, will be a violent one. Someone will hit you on the head or firebomb your car – something to wake you up to the fact that you are not supposed to be here. From the third step you do not recover. That's why you pay tribute, for the protection, for the exclusive franchise.*

(Vito mentioned that Paterno could offer protection in the event of trouble

---

* "An effective threat of punishment is much cheaper than punishment itself, although should actual punishment never occur, the threat may become incredible. The trick is to keep the actual use of force as infrequent as possible. For these reasons it is rewarding to a person of high status that others should avoid challenging his power at all, and his display of appropriate symbols may render a challenge less probable. Like the proclamation of a norm, it renders less likely any challenge made by inadvertence, by lack of awareness on the part of a challenger of the risk he runs" (Homans, 1974, p. 213).

with the authorities. His central position, as a patron, puts him in contact with a vast network of persons, both criminal and legitimate.)

You pay tribute money to make sure that you have an exclusive right to the area, and in the event of trouble Paterno could reach into the prosecutor's office. There are a lot of things that can be done by Paterno to help his people. If you identify me as the person who cashed a stolen check, if you are the only one between me and freedom, your family could be researched through word of mouth: "Who does he know? Who are his relatives? Who does he work for, and what bowling club does he belong to?" We find somebody who knows you, a family member or friend – somebody we can reach and ask to talk to you. He is induced to go to you and say: "Howard, you're a witness against this guy, a friend of some friends of mine. All you have to say is that you're not sure it's him. You will be doing me a favor. I know these people; they don't mean any harm. Who is really going to be hurt, the insurance company that covers the bank. What do you give a shit for them. Just say that when you first saw him, you thought it was the guy. But now, when you are close up, you ain't so sure. That's all you have to say, okay? Then there is reasonable doubt, and the guy walks. You'll be a big man; they owe you a favor whenever you might need one." The amount of pressure that would be placed upon a witness depends on the seriousness of the offense. As Paterno would say: "The guy could take a vacation and never come back." The implications are obvious.

I was not aware of Paterno being invoved in elections, but there is no question that Paterno's tentacles reached into a lot of governmental places including the Morris County prosecutor's office, the Essex County prosecutor's office, the state board of taxation, and Newark – the city of Newark was absolutely and totally corrupt.

(Joe Paterno's patron was Carlo Gambino. Since telephone calls are easily monitored, contact between patron and client had to be face-to-face.)

In the beginning, when I took trips with Joe into New York City to see the old man, Carlo Gambino, I would be told how to conduct myself. "This is how you got to dress: this is how you got to act: keep your mouth shut; don't ask any questions, and don't make any comments unless you are addressed." Although there were some exceptions, most of the meetings took place in an automobile. The first meeting I attended, my first experience with Gambino, took place in a car. Paterno was seeking advice from Gambino on what he should do about a $25,000 fine that was still pending against him from his conviction. Gambino advised him to file a plea in federal court, a sworn statement that he did not have sufficient assets at this point in time to pay the fine. Although this was clearly a legal problem, Joe came to Gambino as opposed to a lawyer. Gambino advised Joe to have his attorney file such a plea in an effort to exonerate (sic) the fine. Gambino was Joe's absolute mentor, and anything that affected Joe could also affect Gambino.

Gambino always made sure that his movements were hard to follow. He always wanted the car moving during these meetings and was very aware if he was possibly being followed. One time, in Joe's Cadillac, Joe, Charlie, and I went to a steak house on West 52nd Street in New York City. We double-parked and Charlie got out and went into the steak house. He came out with Gambino and another person who was with Gambino — I don't know if his name was ever mentioned. I tagged him mentally, in my own mind, with the name "Silent Sam" because he never said anything. Everyone got into the car; Charlie was driving and Paterno sat in the back next to Gambino and Silent Sam. I was in the front with Charlie and was not formally introduced to Gambino, although he acknowledged my presence by a nod of the head.

The conversation, which was conducted in English, concerned Joe's fine. However, there was some additional conversation about what I thought was a rather insignificant item, and it was conducted in Italian. I felt that it was an item that you usually don't bother the boss with. I compared it with a legitimate business where the unit manager or a section chief or division manager does not take everything to higher management; there are some things that you make decisions about yourself.* The issue being discussed in Italian concerned an individual known as Jonsie who was operating a Shylock business in the Ironbound section of Newark, a heavily industrialized, blue-collar area. Jonsie worked for Paterno, and Joe suspected that he was now loaning out his own money as opposed to working with Paterno's: he was apparently going into business for himself. Joe asked Gambino how he should handle it. Since Jonsie was a low, street-level fellow, I thought that Paterno should have handled it directly himself; the man worked for him. However, Gambino said that he would take care of it, and I never knew what actually had happened. However, at a later meeting with Gambino, Joe advised the old man that things were working out well with Jonsie; that was all he said. Now that can mean an awful lot. Those few words meant that the guy was falling into line — doing what he was supposed to be doing — that there were no further problems with him.

---

* An article in the New York Times ("Informer Glad to Help F.B.I.," 1980) discussed the conviction of Joe Bonanno (his first for a felony) in federal court for "obstructing justice." The central witness against Bonanno and his associates, a legitimate California automobile dealer, is quoted as saying: "Sometimes I wonder why they call it organized crime. They were terrible businessmen. It took them six months to make decisions that I would make in six minutes" (p. 61).

During the entire meeting we drove in and out of side streets, a security precaution, for a total of about 15 minutes. We then turned back and let Gambino and his man out on the corner of 52nd Street and, I believe, 6th Avenue (Avenue of the Americas). We returned to New Jersey. During the ride home there was no discussion of the prior conversation with Gambino.

During other meetings with Gambino one of the first things that Joe did was to hand the old man an envelope, an envelope that I presume contained money. Gambino, without even looking at it, would merely hand it over to Silent Sam who would put it in the breast pocket of his sports jacket. I guess this was Joe's tribute to Gambino. There were actually two types of meetings: advisory and informative. In the first type, Joe would be asking advice from Gambino; in the second type, he would update him on events of mutual concern. Their conversations were always guarded; that is, they would not mention directly names, dates, and places. A conversation between Paterno and Gambino might come out: "You know that fellow we talked about in Bloomfield? Well, everything is okay," or, "We're going to have problems with him." I don't know if this was done to keep me out, but I doubt it, since it would have been easier just not to take me along; what did Paterno have to take me along for anyway? I believe that this is just the way they were accustomed to communicating: speaking in a guarded way as an additional safety device in case they were being overheard, being taped. But, in fact, they understood each other and had no need to mention an individual's name.*

I was absolutely and totally forbidden by Joe to ever mention the name Gambino to anyone; I could not mention it to a soul: "Anybody asks you who you are with, or you get into some kind of problem, you say you're with us," meaning Paterno. "But, you never take it further; you don't say you are with Gambino." This was an absolute "no no," and it clearly carried with it the threat of mayhem for disobedience. The rule was obviously to add additional insulation for Gambino, to protect him from any prosecution. For example, let's go back to the situation with the wristwatch and "Jerry the Jew." I told Jerry that I was with Paterno. If I had told him that I was with Gambino, I doubt that it would have had any greater effect. But suppose Jerry got nailed for something and to save his own skin he starts to open up. "Yeah. I know this guy Vito, he's into 'paper,' he's their paperman, he's with

---

* This manner of dialogue requires a variation of what Goffman (1974, chap. 3) refers to as keying, without which those listening will not be able to adequately interpret the transaction. Giddens (1976) notes that "in everyday situations of interaction the will to speak is also sometimes the will to baffle, puzzle, deceive, to be misunderstood" (p. 105).

Gambino." Now, if Jerry decides to open up, he cannot implicate, or even mention, Gambino. The best he can do is mention Paterno.*

Law enforcement people are successful in dealing with organized criminal activities to the extent that they are able to get information, primarily through informants. They supply the authorities with a constant array of facts and semifacts that law enforcement people, over a period of time, are able to piece together. Although they may not even be able to make a case, they get a hell of a picture of what's going on in the street — what's happening in organized crime. You can't get all of the information from any single informant, a guy like Valachi, for example. It's impossible, because he's a street soldier and he doesn't know that much. The same with me — I don't know much, only a tiny segment. But, you keep putting these segments together and pretty soon you get a hell of a good picture. Although the picture might be said to be somewhat speculative, it's more factual than it is speculative.

It's a funny thing, but on a number of occasions when Joe met with Gambino, I felt like I was a bump on a log: I had absolutely no relationship to anything that they were discussing. For all intents and purposes I had no business being there; it was kind of like being privy to a domestic dispute; you feel that you should not be paying attention. However, I spent a lot of time with Joe and he would say: "I want you to take a ride with me to New York City to meet someone." I never questioned it. Although we never explicitly discussed it, I believe that Joe was taking me along as a way of grooming me for membership in the organization, the Gambino family.

(Observers have questioned whether it is more advantageous to be a member or an associate of an organized crime family.)

A member of the organization is an insider, and he gets fringe benefits. For example, he could take advantage of a robbery by funding it, putting up the front money to get the project off the ground. The Campisis robbed a payroll from a Pathmark Supermarket. The inside information that they had proved to be wrong: instead of $100,000, there was only $50,000, but that's beside the point. For them to get the show on the road, there has to be research; things have to be done. You just don't rip off a payroll like that without research; it's not like robbing a 7-Eleven Store. You have to know

---

* This "rule" probably dates back to the 1930s and the serious legal difficulties encountered by Lucky Luciano. In 1936 Luciano was convicted of compulsory prostitution and sentenced to a term of 30 to 50 years. Although Luciano apparently had no direct involvement in the activity, some of his henchmen, using his name, organized and extorted significant sums from brothels in New York City.

delivery times – who is involved, how many guards, whether they are all armed; where the money goes when it leaves the truck and enters the building and whether there will be broads involved, because if there are, you may have to deal with screaming. You've got to have a lot of information. You also have to be able to get away safely. This requires at least three cars: one for the robbery (a stolen car), a crash car to follow you and intercept (crash into) any cops that are pursuing (a legitimate car) and, finally, a car to change over to and a change of clothes. This all requires money, R&D, research and development. An insider could fund that kind of an operation.

This kind of operation might take $5,000 or $10,000 and several weeks of research, or more. The Campisis would not go to a small fish, to an independent. To do that they would have to get permission because you are talking about a big robbery; you are talking about something that will cause a lot of waves. Someone might get killed; and, in this case, someone, a guard, did get killed. When you kill somebody, especially if it's a guard who, even though he is not a law enforcement officer in a strict sense, is there to enforce the law, protect the money, there is going to be a lot of heat. With these risks you have to go to someone like Paterno. You tell him that there is a payroll you want to hit, and you explain the risks and ask for his OK. For this, he, Paterno, gets tribute, because he will have to suffer some from the heat that can be generated by a big robbery in his territory.

Let me give you another example of opportunities as a result of being a member, a true insider. You might know someone in a stock brokerage house who can rip off $0.5 million worth of blue chip stock, bearer bonds, negotiable items. But, this guy wants $10,000 or $20,000 from you upon delivery of the package. If I am a "wise guy," you come to me and I'm going to give you the money.* If you need $20,000, I'll get it for you to give to your connection. You come to me because you know I can get the money and that I'm not going to turn you into the law. I am also protected. I don't want to know anything about what happened to the deal. If it didn't go down, I don't want to know the reason – I want my $20,000 back. Or, if the deal does go down, I want my 5 or 10 percent over and above the $20,000 front money. I've got a guarantee, I'm a member of the organization.† I don't care if you have to steal the money from your mother – that's your problem. You either give me my piece of the action, or you are not going to be around anymore.

---

* Wise guy is a term used to designate a member of organized crime. Other terms include made guy or our friend.

† Organized crime serves to reduce the uncertainty, hence the risk, inherent in criminal endeavors.

That's how simple it is. That's why the organization has "policemen," guys like "Butch."*

One thing that always disturbed me is that if you are a member of the organization, you could be asked to do something that you did not want to do; it was against your morals, or whatever you got. For myself, there are some things that I just would not do for love or for money, or for the organization. If you told me to break someone's legs, a complete stranger, or to hit, murder a guy, I couldn't do it.† But, just like in any big business organization, they got guys with expertise for that kind of thing.

[What are the functional or working roles in organized crime that you are familiar with as a result of your experiences, including your own role?]

I was introduced a few times to people I didn't know as "our paperman"; Joe Paterno simply said: "This is Vitone, and he's our paperman." That would mean to you that if you had a pocketful of stolen paper and didn't know how the hell to get rid of it, didn't know how to convert it into cash, that I'm the expert in this field. I'm the one who knows what I am doing, and the fact that Paterno introduced me to you automatically puts a stamp of approval on me: I am a stand-up person — if the whistle blows, I'm gonna take the fall and not implicate anyone else. I would also, on occasion, be used as an adviser. Among higher-echelon mafia you have counselors, people who advise them. But, I did not have that role on any kind of permanent basis.

I have heard the term enforcer used, and Joe introduced me to a guy named Butch as "our enforcer." A few years later, a guy who was with the Campisi family was pointed out to me as a hit man. He was then introduced to me by someone in the Campisi organization as "our hit man." Now enforcer and hit man are basically interchangeable — the enforcer being the more sophisticated term for a person prone to violent activity, resolving issues by violence. The hit man is the cruder term meaning the same thing. The word enforcer has the connotation that he enforces the law, like a policeman enforces the law, except that it's a different law. An enforcer might also be a street soldier, a low-ranking member of the organization who handles the violence on a regular basis.

Joe's prime enforcer was a fellow I mentioned before, Butch — I don't recall his last name. At the time that I first became exposed to Butch, I got

---

* "Butch" has been identified by law enforcement officials as Frank Micelli, a New Jersey enforcer for the Gambino family.

†Vito is asserting that he had not fully internalized the values of organized crime.

the impression that he was on Joe's payroll, just like Charlie Apple. This meant that Butch was available to Joe anytime that Joe picks up the telephone. These occasions in my experience were not a daily or even a weekly kind of occurrence. As Joe became bigger and had his tentacles into many things, the relationship between him and Butch became much closer; there was more contact between the two of them. Like I said, it's an insurance policy kind of thing – you pay the premium and you hope you never need the insurance, but it's there if you need it. (Would Butch be involved in the type of enforcement that required a murder?) Absolutely. Paterno said many times: "If so and so gets out of line, we'll hit him. I'll send Butch; we got Butch in the wings." This would be the bottom line – if an individual were to get out of line to such a degree that this was the only course of action. (Were you ever privy to such a situation?) No, not directly, for several reasons, and I'm not trying to cover up here because that would be ludicrous at this point in time. I was not known to advocate violence; it was generally known that this was not my bag, not my sort of thing. I always felt that you could talk to people, reason with them. But Paterno did not accept that philosophy; he believed that there are times when only violence will work, that many individuals only understand violence. You have to understand that for a person of Paterno's stature to want to kill somebody, that's the last resort. The guy has already been spoken to, he has already been warned – the violence is a result of disobedience.

The first time that I heard the term <u>money-mover</u> was when I was introduced to Meyer Lansky by Joe Paterno, when he was with Carlo Gambino. I was introduced to him as Meyer, and we shook hands: "Hello. How are you? It's nice to meet you." And that was the end of the conversation. Later, on the way home from New York City to New Jersey, Joe said: "Meyer, he's a money-mover." I didn't know exactly what that meant at the time. I conjured up a picture in my own mind, which turned out to be accurate, that he had the ability to handle large sums of illicit money. He could move it through various channels and pump it back into legitimate business. Another guy, later on, was introduced to me by Joe as a money-mover – his name was Howard, and like Lansky he was a Jewish fellow. He got Joe involved in some very lucrative real estate transactions in the Jersey area, in New York City as well as upstate New York, along the Hudson, Spring Valley, and places like that. He also involved Joe heavily in real estate in Florida. Howard was in the real estate business, the money-broker business, or something like that. Again, it's something that you don't ask; if it's volunteered, or if you hear something, okay. But, you just don't ask.*

---

* Undercover investigator (New York City Police Department) Doug Le Vien states that in organized crime you never ask questions about anything: "When you're dealing with high-level Cosa Nostra, especially, you never ask

VITO: AN ILLUSTRATIVE CASE STUDY

You also don't ask for surnames. The weirdest thing is that in organized crime you can know an individual for years by nothing more than his first name or his nickname. I don't believe that I ever knew the real name of Charlie Apple. He was an old-time friend and traveling companion, a street soldier who was very close with Paterno; where you saw Paterno, you saw Charlie Apple. Yet, I never knew him by anything other than Charlie Apple. The patriarch of the Campisi family was Anthony Campisi, but he was always called Nanay; that's what you called him. His son and nephew were Petey White and Petey Black, because although they were both named Peter, one was swarthy and had a dark complexion and the other was quite light. You could know someone for years and years and you never asked for a surname.

EXITING FROM ORGANIZED CRIME

It was my association with Mike Mariani that brought my first and only criminal conviction. It happened quite stupidly; I should have known better, but I didn't — boy, have I heard that before. One day Mike and I went to Newark Airport where he had previously worked as a baggage handler, freight handler; he knew the airport inside out. I went there with him for the purpose of looking over some new refuse containers that had been purchased by the airport. I thought that they might be of use in my garbage collection business. Mike, without alerting me, went there to steal mail. When I told Mike about the containers and said that they were at the food-processing area, he said he knew how to get me into that parking lot so that I would be right on top of the containers. I would not have to get lost in the shuffle and hubbub of the airport. However, after I parked the car, Mike said he was going over to get a mail bag. "Let's not screw around, Mike. Let me get a look at the garbage containers and then let's just go." He just looked at me in a puzzled kind of way: "Vito, it's as easy as taking candy from a baby. There's nothing to it. These people don't have nobody around. I can hop the fence and go faster than I'm talking to you." With that he ran out and scaled the fence. When he got to the mail platform, the receiving area for mail coming in on airplanes, he grabbed a bag at random and reapproached the fence; we're talking about 75 to 100 feet away. He threw the bag over the

---

where you come from or what you do. If he tells me, 'I can reach a judge if you do what you gotta do, it would be out of the norm for me to ask what the judge's name is." If, on the other hand, he is suspicious of you, "he's gonna ask you who's your mother and who's your grandmother. And that test you'll never pass" if you are a police officer (Edelman, 1980, p. 48).

Le Vien's work resulted in the successful prosecution of several important organized crime figures including Paul Vario and Carmine Trumanti (boss of the Lucchese family).

fence and yelled to me: "Get if off the ground. Put in in the car." I was hesitant; this was stupid and I was scared to death. The dummy that I was, I got out of the car, picked up the bag, and threw it into the car.

We both got back into the car and as I was pulling out of the parking lot, I looked into the rear-view mirror. "Oh shit, there's a police car behind us." It was unmarked, but there were two guys in it, and it was the heat. I glanced around. "Mike, somebody's on our butt." He tells me to turn down the next aisle like we are looking for a parking spot, but the car is still behind us. For a few more minutes we maneuver in and of parking aisles. Suddenly, two Port of New York Authority marked police cars with their lights on converge on us. "Get rid of that fuckin' bag," I screamed at Mike. "Throw it under another car, but get it out of here." It was too late and they were on us. I pulled over, but they did not know whether we were armed. They yanked us out of the car, pulled us by the back of the collar, and threw us up against the car: "Spread your legs. Put your hands on the roof of the car." And then the body search. We were roughed up, handcuffed, and thrown into the back of one police car. We were driven to a federal building and turned over to the postal inspectors; it was a federal rap. We spent the night in a holding cell that the city of Newark apparently leases to the federal government.

I called my brother and told him what had happened. He was shocked but didn't argue about the role he would have to play. He would be there for the arraignment the next morning and would make sure that there was a bail bondsman there as well as an attorney. I was released on personal recognizance because I was a homeowner who had no previous record. Mike Mariani, who had a long record, was held in lieu of $2,500 bail. For some reason, and I never did understand why, the newspapers picked up on this situation: "Local Contractor Arrested in Alleged Mail Theft." They didn't blast it on page one, but they did not bury it either. It stood out: name, address, refuse contractor, and so on. It wasn't that kind of crime, so I still don't know why they picked up on it. Anyway, it hurt my family; it hurt my kids most of all. They were poked fun of at school: "You know your mafia father got caught; he's nothing but a thief" – that kind of crap. I could take it, but when your family has to be hurt, that's rough. It's embarrassing, let's face it.

My lawyer separated my case from Mike Mariani's since he pled guilty and got a reduced sentence. He could have picked up five and, instead, got two years in Danbury (Correctional Facility in Connecticut). I had in fact thrown the bag into my car at the request of Mike, but it was not my intent to go to Newark Airport to steal anything. I felt that I had a chance to walk. I attempted to reach Mike through his wife and have him appear in my defense at the trial. He would do it – for a price. The price was $10,000. His family was destitute, on welfare and really down. He saw $10,000 as giving them $100 a week while he was away for two years. I could understand this, but when I told my attorney he would not go for it. But, I kept trying. I was not on Mike's visitor list, and I didn't want to be. I told his wife that I would give her $1,000 down and that after he makes his statement, she would be given the balance. In the meantime, I will give the balance to my lawyer to hold. Mike wouldn't go for it, and I went on trial. The jury did not buy my story. After being out about six hours, they returned a verdict of guilty. I was hoping for at least a hung jury, but I didn't even get that. The judge wanted a presentence report from the probation department before he would hand down a sentence. We asked for a continuance of bail, based on the fact that we wanted to file an appeal. During the appeal process the presentence report was completed, and I received a six-month sentence and a $2,500 fine. I never did the six months, nor did I ever pay the fine. I also continued to work the check scheme.

However, things had changed. I was agonizing mentally over my plight. I was most concerned about the shame I had brought on my family. There's just no way you can make up for that kind of situation. I began to reflect on my situation and my past activities: Was I really benefiting by all of this? Was my family benefiting? A beautiful home and a nice surrounding, but . . . I was asking myself questions like: Couldn't I have gotten this without dirtying myself? At the same time trouble was coming from Uncle Sam – the criminal division of the Internal Revenue Service (IRS). They had subpoenaed my books and my financial records and were tearing my returns to pieces. They had assigned this Italian guy to my case, and he was thorough as he was vindictive; I was in trouble. There was no way in hell that I could cover up or justify the tax on my income for too many years. I was going to get hurt; they were making a criminal investigation, not a civil. Civil I could handle. "It's money, okay. You want money, fine me and you will get the money." If they had taken that route, maybe my thinking would have changed, but they didn't. Quite frankly, of all enforcement agencies, the IRS frightened me more than any other. I remembered how they audited my father's books, and he was legit. The horrors they put him through, and they were approaching him from a routine normal audit. They were not approaching me that way.

All this stuff was running through my head, and it all boiled down to two choices. I could either cop out to the whole situation and take what was coming, come out of jail, or maybe not even go to jail except for the six months, and start anew. Maybe we would move to another area where I was not known, where my family would not have to be embarrassed. I could use my connections to go back into business. This would be the "man's" way out; this would be the way that a supposed macho man would take – a stand-up guy. You take the blows and you keep your mouth shut. That's one of the rules. I started to search my mind for alternatives.

I went to the FBI office in Morristown, New Jersey. In return for helping them, I wanted my legal problems to be taken care of. It could not be revealed that I had informed – this would save my face and my life. "I know you guys can't make any promises," I said, "and I am willing to do the six months on the mail theft rap. But, I want the IRS off my back, and I don't want any other problems. When it's all over, I just want to drift away. I will sell my business and drift away, put down roots someplace else. I can't do that if it becomes known that I was an informant."

(Vito provided a great deal of information to the Justice Department. Some of this information resulted in several indictments, including that of a hit man. However, it turned out that the Justice Department also needed his testimony to ensure a conviction.)

WITNESS PROTECTION PROGRAM

When I arrived at the Strike Force office,* I was told that there was no way to protect my anonymity. I was going to have to testify, and I was offered two choices: take it on the run, on my own, or let us relocate you and give you a new identity. This was the first time that I had heard of the Witness Protection Program. The word relocation hit me like a sledge hammer. I had not even considered this alternative; I believed that my identity would be protected. But, the bottom line was that they wanted a conviction more than they wanted to protect my role. I was naive.

Late that afternoon, I came home with a half-dozen U.S. marshals. They concocted a story for the benefit of my family that I had been actively engaged in undercover work for various enforcement agencies in the federal government for a long period of time. This helped me save face with my family. It also masked the mail theft situation, because my involvement in the mail theft was supposedly to get me in better with mobsters, and that I really was not a thief. My family totally and completely believed what was said – because they wanted to believe it. They wanted to believe that their husband and father was not a criminal, not a thief or "wise guy." Deep down inside I felt that they were not believing this tale, but it offered an excuse. To firm it up I had the FBI agents come to the house and talk to my family. I told my wife that I had been involved in a great deal of undercover activity on a patriotic basis and that there would be a couple of guys who would be coming pretty soon to explain the whole situation. "Let's wait for them," I suggested, because I did not want to start telling stories that might conflict with the stories the agents were going to tell. I called my brother and asked him to come over to the house, because it had been explained to me that we were going to leave, disappear.

---

* The Strike Force was developed under Robert Kennedy when he was attorney general. It is designed to coordinate and integrate federal (and sometimes local) efforts to combat organized crime. Strike Force units were set up in all major cities where the type of organized crime being discussed in this study is known to exist.

We could not be moved out overnight as the marshals had indicated. They had a personnel problem; there were some civil disorders or something in Washington and thousands of people had been arrested. Many of the marshals were assigned to deal with the situation and were not available to help move us out.Because of the delay, we had an advantage that many other relocated witnesses apparently do not have. They are simply picked up and taken away overnight, which doesn't allow them any time whatsoever to plan for what is being left behind. In my situation there was a lot being left behind. I had a business, real estate, and a house. Since they would not allow the kids to go to school anymore, they yanked the school records. There were little things like providing for the care of several cats and a dog. I was able to sit down with my attorney and transferred everything to him to dispose of by power of attorney.

After about two weeks under guard in our own house, we were moved to Washington, D.C., by airplane. I was using a fictitious name. After one night in a Washington motel, we were driven to a place in Maryland just outside of Annapolis and housed in a motel for almost nine weeks. There were six people in two rooms, and this left a lot to be desired. We looked upon it as a temporary inconvenience, and it was very expensive for the government. We ate out three meals every day. Whenever any of us ventured out to buy a newspaper or toilet articles, marshals accompanied us. At this time the government was picking up the tab for everything. The marshals told us that they would help me to get a job, change our names, and provide us new identification, in addition to finding us new housing. However, to get these things was like pulling teeth from a hen, which, as you are aware, has no teeth.

After almost nine weeks we were relocated to Columbia, South Carolina, where we lived in garden apartment complex. The 24-hour protection ceased, and we were devoid of all identification except for our original documents, which, of course, would be too dangerous to use. They had given us a name out of the air, a cover name, a code name, which was "Domino." So we put that name on our mailbox and became known as the Domino family. They continued to pay the rent, but we were reduced to $75 a week for our table and personal use. I picked this up in cash every week from the U.S. marshal in Columbia. At the same time I was in touch almost daily with Bob Richardson (the U.S. attorney) in Newark. I was asking, in fact begging, for the process to unfold and reach its ultimate conclusion.

Although I kept asking, I was not told how they would get me a job, and I found out that the United States Marshals Service is very ineffective when it comes to helping a witness. The simple truth is that as a street person, as a guy who was into criminal activity, I can produce identification ten times faster than the marshals, and mine will stand up. I'm talking about birth certificates, school records, and Social Security cards. It took the marshals weeks to produce that type of documentation. And what are you supposed to do until then? You are, in effect, a nonperson. If you use your real name, then everybody and his brother knows who you are and where you're from. You are opening the door for being found, and the one thing that they made clear is that they do not want you to be found.

You have to completely sever every single relationship or association that you had, other than with the immediate members of your family. Even then, you communicate through a third party, through the marshals' office, which supplies a mail drop. In my situation they failed to even provide that. When dealing with your relatives, you have to be very careful; you cannot tell them where you are. You say that you are "down South" instead of saying Columbia. It's not that you are afraid that they are going to tell the wrong people, but information often gets dropped innocently. It's particularly hard on the kids because they have school friends they would like to write to or telephone, and you cannot let them. They just have to forget it, wipe the slate clear. We did that very well, I believe. The only people I communicated with were my mother and brother (Vito's father was deceased) and my attorney. My wife did the same. We wanted to protect ourselves. Yet, if someone were really looking for us very hard, we could have been found. This is because the government did not have funds for us to deal with such items as transportation. In a suburban or rural area, a car is a must; yet we had no car, and there was no public transportation. The stores were too far to walk to, but when we asked the marshals what to do, they just shrugged their shoulders. "What the hell am I supposed to do? You told me to sell my car." The answer turned out, to my way of thinking, to be an invitation: "I don't know. You'll have to find a way." They way I found was simple.

I had gone in and out of the federal building in Columbia many times, often with marshals. I found out that there was a motor pool for agents, marshals, and other government officials. Very nonchalantly, I just walked into the basement of the federal building, into the parking lot, and drove out with a motor pool car. I went right past the guard who knew my face and assumed that I was a federal agent since I was often with the marshals. I just waved to him and drove out. I figured that the worst they could do was what they did – nothing. After about a week of using the government's car, which also included the credit card attached to the key chain to buy gasoline, one of the marshals asked me: "Vito, how did you get here today." They had been sending somebody to pick me up whenever I came to get my allowance. "Oh, I drove in – in one of your cars," I answered nonchalantly. "Oh – what? One of our cars? What do you mean?" I told him the simple truth: "I went downstairs and took a car from the motor pool. I've been using it since last week." After the look of astonishment: "You're kidding, right?" I said: "I'm using your friggin' car, and I'm going to continue using it." "Oh no," he said, "you can't do that. You're not a government employee. If you had an accident, there would be a lot of red tape, complications." I conned him into allowing me to use the car for a few more days. Realizing that they would eventually take the car away from me, I turned it in and went over to an alternate plan. Using my own credit card in the name of Palermo, I rented an automobile. Of course I was never going to be known by that name any more, and I had no intention of paying for the rental — how could they find me? I used the car for about five months; as far as I know, Uncle Sam never paid for it either. Of course, this was a dangerous move, using my real name — but what can you do?

Employment

The government also failed to provide me with a background that I could use to find a job, so I designed one. I fabricated a résumé with education and work background and submitted it to Bob Richardson and Gerald Shur, who I believe was the alleged liason between the criminal division of the Justice Department and the United States Marshals Service. I say "alleged" because at that time it seemed that he really ran the whole show with respect to the protection program. I wrote: "Since you have failed to provide me with the promised background, in order to get a job I have manufactured the attached résumé." I asked if he agreed with it and would he support it? I received no reply, which to me meant implied consent. I began to apply for jobs.

The résumé that I prepared stated that I had been employed in a family-owned and -operated business, a large northern New Jersey waste collection company. After many years, it stated, I went into business on my own, and I used my attorney and my brother as references. The résumé said that I eventually sold this business and took a job with the Bureau of Solid Wastes, a federal agency. I started out as the person who established guidelines for disposal facilities. These guidelines, I wrote, were ultimately adopted by the Environmental Protection Agency. The résumé continued that over the next few years I received promotions to — I forget the title that I gave myself — administrative director or something like that (it sounded good). I gave myself a line of progression leading up to this position. I also noted that during the last few years that I was with the Bureau of Solid Wates, when it was incorporated into the Office of Solid Waste Management, I was "loaned," and I put quotation marks around the word loaned, to the U.S. Department of Justice. The Department of Justice, I said, was making a probe of possible infiltration of mob elements into the private sector of solid waste management. Now this gave it an air of mystery, and the bottom line was that due to the sensitive nature of my employment, I am unable to elaborate beyond this point. I concluded by stating that I was seeking employment on a stationary basis, that I was tired of traveling around, tired of uprooting my family. I was looking for a stable position. I also listed as my references several federal agents and my brother.

My résumé also indicated that I had a Bachelor of Science degree in business management from the Wharton School of Business (University of Pennsylvania) — why not the best? Some employers were looking for a person with an engineering degree, but there was no way I could fake that. I did not have the knowledge in math and related areas to get away with that. In addition, to be a "P.E.," a professional engineer, tests had to be passed. I felt that I was qualified in the management of solid waste systems, particularly in the public sector, where I had experience and knowledge in the operation of municipalities in northern New Jersey. I knew the bureaucracy in solid waste management. Using leads from trade publications, I began sending out the résumé. The government paid for transportation costs, and a marshal always accompanied me when I traveled for a job interview.

(Vito was quite successful in securing important and well-paying positions both in the private and public sector. However, during his last job he had been "uncovered" and was now in North Carolina very bitter about the lack of help he was getting from the government.) *

---

* The inadequacies of the Witness Protection Program are discussed in a New York Times Magazine article concerned with the tribulations of a noncriminal prosecution witness and her family. (This case was also the subject of a "60 Minutes" television story broadcast on February 4, 1979.) All of Vito's complaints are supported in the article (Mitchell, 1980).

8

Interpretation and Implications

VITO AS DEVIANT

Vito is an improbable organized crime figure: he does not come from a deprived environment, his family has not been involved in criminal activities, and his childhood was not particularly troubled. Vito graduated from high school, was not involved with juvenile gangs or street groups, and had the opportunity to attend college like his older brother. His blue-collar experience in the refuse business and his southern Italian heritage provide some background, but it is actually his white-collar knowledge and lack of scruples that make him useful to persons in organized crime. The techniques of a paperman are of his own design: Vito does research, reading books on banking procedures and "picking the brains" of bank employees. He appears to view his illegal activities as more or less an extension of his legitimate business. Thrasher (1968), writing in 1927, noted that in some cases persons in organized crime "seem to be men of questionable ethics who come from presumedly reputable or well-to-do families, but who have been drawn into the activities of organized crime" (p. 286).

Vito identifies with "con men types" such as Mattie Brown and even Charles Ponzi. When I asked Vito if any books or movies about crime or criminals had an impact on him, he quickly recalled: "<u>Famous Frauds</u> — it related to stories about the great con men and swindlers throughout history. One I can remember was Ponzi. He was the great pyramid scheme builder who acquired investor's money and paid off later investors with some of the first money and was eventually caught."* Despite his identification with con

---

*Vito is incorrect. Starting in 1919, Charles Ponzi, an ex-convict, bilked millions from gullible investors in what came to be known as a "pyramid" or "Ponzi" scheme. Money is secured for investment purposes, but it is not invested. "Profits" are paid out from the funds of new investors, and the scheme runs out when there are insufficient new investors.

men types, Vito distinguishes between himself and "the criminal element," "full-fledged criminals, people who devote all of their time and energy to criminal pursuits." He expresses disapproval of physical violence, "a stupid turn-off," and generally resists the deviant label. Thus, he is quite upset when the newspapers report his arrest for mail theft: "The meaningful issue is whether the activity, or any of my activities can stand for me, or be regarded as proper indications of my being. I have done a theft, been signified a thief; am I a thief?" (Matza, 1969, p. 170). To accept thief as concept of self, Matza adds that the actor must unify "doing" (theft) with "being" (a thief). Vito is unwilling to take this final step.

This attitude contrasts with his apparent enjoyment of the mafioso role in his community of Mason. Ball (1970) notes that we are under constant pressure to present appearances indicative of respectability (p. 345). There is, however, an alternative approach: "to promote redefinition so as to obviate the need for concealment and falsity" (p. 347). By this approach, Ball argues, the otherwise nonrespectable can avoid negative consequences. Actors may be able to count on the generalization of their lack of respectability to other areas and thereby provide audiences with explanations, interpretations, and meanings for otherwise apparently dissonant actions (p. 365).* Vito is simply inconsistent: he seeks to take advantage of the positive aspects of a deviant role (that is, acceptance by Joe Paterno) while never quite defining himself as deviant. Goffman (1973) writes that

> while we can expect to find natural movement back and forth between cynicism and sincerity, still we must not rule out the kind of

---

*This is vividly portrayed in an essay by social critic Tom Wolfe (1970):

And now, in the season of Radical Chic, the Black Panthers. That huge Panther there, the one Felicia is smiling her tango smile at, is Robert Bay, who just forty-one hours ago was arrested in an altercation with the police, supposedly over a .38 caliber revolver. . . . And now he is out on bail and walking into Leonard and Felicia Bernstein's thirteen-room penthouse duplex on Park Avenue. Harassment & Hassels, Guns & Pigs, Jail & Bail – they're real, these Black Panthers. The very idea of them, these real revolutionaries, who actually put their lives on the line, runs through Lenny's duplex like a rogue hormone. Everyone casts a glance, or stares, or tries a smile, and then sizes up the house for the somehow delicious counterpoint. (P. 6)

If Wolfe were at a lawn party in Mason, perhaps he could have made a similar observation about "Mafia Chic."

transitional point that can be sustained on the strength of a little self-illusion. We find that the individual may attempt to induce the audience to judge him and the situation in a particular way, and he may seek this judgment as an ultimate end in itself, and yet he may not completely believe that he deserves the valuation of self which he asks for or that the impression of reality that he fosters is valid. (P. 21)

Vito's family also exists in the penumbra of deviance, realizing that Vito must be involved in criminal activities and, yet, not wanting to know – as if to know is to define as deviant.

It is not until his arrest for mail theft that there is a real crisis – being officially labeled as deviant – and his family must suffer the indignity of societal reaction. With the connivance of federal officials, Vito tries to ease the crisis with a story that portrays him as an undercover operative, not a criminal. Vito points out, however, that his family believed the story because they wanted to believe it.

For many years Vito was able to live in two worlds, belonging fully to neither, a "marginal man": "a cultural hybrid on the verge of two different patterns of life, not knowing to which of them he belongs" (Schutz, 1971, p. 104). Durkheim (1951) tells us: "The more weakened the groups to which he belongs, the less he depends on them, the more he consequently depends only on himself and recognizes no other rules of conduct other than what are founded on his private interests" (p. 209). Vito explains, however, that he became an informer because his attitude had undergone change over time. At one point, he insists, he was completely prepared to accept the rules of organized crime, to be a stand-up guy. When the crisis occurs, Vito is not (at least at that time) prepared to suffer the sanctions that were in store (the legal and the label) for mail theft and income tax evasion. Instead, he opted for the straight world, extricated himself from a deviant status as best he could under the circumstances, and at considerable risk to his personal safety. Becker (1973) believes:

Apprehension may not lead to increasing deviance if the situation in which the individual is apprehended for the first time occurs at a point where he can still choose between alternate lines of action. Faced, for the first time, with the possible ultimate and drastic consequences of what he is doing, he may decide that he does not want to take the deviant road, and turn back. (P. 37)

After completing this section, I realized that I had not given Vito an opportunity to offer his version of his concept of self; that perhaps my interpretation would be at odds with his own view. Accordingly, I wrote to Vito. On April 25, 1980, I received the following (unedited) reply:

Did I view myself as a criminal and/or a businessman with illegal activities? The answer is a complex one, I guess. I knew what was right and wrong. I knew what was legal and illegal. I knew that what I was doing was in fact illegal. It was looked upon by me as a game. My wits and brains against theirs. The good guys vs. the bad guys. Since I did not participate on a full time basis or make my total living from illegal activities, I never really looked upon myself as a criminal. If I could get away with it and not get nailed it was OK with me. In addition if I could shield my family from these elements and keep from them the knowledge of my activities I felt comfortable.

At any rate thanks for letting me offer my views. In sum, I never really viewed myself as a criminal, then or now.

Ditton (1974) points out that Vito's concept of self is a characteristic of "part-time crime." He notes that the crucial difference between the full-time criminal and the part-time one is that the former sees his legitimate occupation as nominal, while the part-time criminal perceives his illegitimate activity as nominal (p. 91). The part-time criminal does not suffer from a criminal self-image but sees his primary deviance – crime – as only a segment of his life.

In theoretical terms, part-time crime may be defined as those forms of criminal activity which are psychologically unaffected by societal reaction, and which eternally retain their primary deviation status in the eyes of practitioners. In this sense, societal reaction does not transform primary into secondary deviance, but instead entrenches it rigidly and ultimately as primary – and part-time. (P. 91)

AN AMERICAN MAFIA

While Vito has never been to Italy, the pattern of operation he describes is quite similar to that of the Sicilian mafia: "My meaning of mafia is that there are in fact a group of people who are tightly knit by virtue of ethnic and family ties who participate in all forms of criminal activity on a highly organized basis." Vito refers to organized crime in the United States as the mafia – this is the term that Joe and Nick Paterno used. In one instance, they both referred to Albert Anastasia as a "mad dog," a killer who made a lot of noise and brought bad publicity to the mafia. The mafia in the United States is thus viewed as an entity that can suffer from "bad publicity"; mafia becomes the Mafia, a criminal society, when persons view themselves as members and act toward it in a stable and relatively orderly manner.

The term don is used when addressing Joe Paterno's father, don Antonio, Carlo Gambino, and Joseph Bonanno. Barzini (1965) reports that don "is the corruption of the Latin dominus. It means a little more than signore. It is used (in Sicily) for noblemen, gentlemen of means, priests, and Mafia leaders" (p. 263). Vito uses the term amici, which also appeared in the "De Cavalcante Tapes." Gli amici is a common term used to describe mafiosi in Sicily. Vito refers several times to the concern with respect – in Sicilian, uomini rispettati ("men who exact respect") are mafiosi. It is part of the southern Italian heritage to want "above all to be obeyed, admired, feared and envied" (p. 236).

The cultural heritage of Sicily provided mafia, and its American manifestation maintains some of the culturally derived terms and organizational structure (Issue one) as well as rules and traditions (Issue two). An alternative proposition is that the news media, newspapers, periodicals, books, movies, and television influence persons in organized crime – a case of life imitating fiction.

We need to consider the extent to which criminals may reflect or even act out roles that are inspired by the popular media. Joey Gallo, a notorious Brooklyn gangster, is known to have copied George Raft and later Richard Widmark when he "played" at being a gangster. Klockars (1974), in his study of a fence, Vincent Swaggi (a pseudonym), notes that Swaggi believed that film characters strongly influence the style if not the techniques of criminals (p. 95). Vito, in his narrative, tells us about Nick Paterno:

> Another thing that tended to lend credence to the mafioso image was Nick Paterno, who often came to visit. Nick drove a big, black Cadillac, and if there is anything to the stereotype of a mafioso-type person, Nick would fall into that category. He dressed like one, he talked like one, and he acted like one. He wore black Italian silk suits and expensive jewelry, diamond pinky rings.

Criminals also read, and some appear to enjoy reading about organized crime. Ianni (1972) reports that one member of the Lupollo family began to refer to the family patriarch as the "Godfather" soon after Mario Puzo's book came out (pp. 112-13). Reuter and Rubinstein (1978b) report that all of their informants have ("alas") read the Valachi Papers or have seen The Godfather (p. 63). I was with Vito one day when he pointed to Gay Talese's (1971) account of Joe Bonanno (Honor Thy Father) in my library and began discussing its central character. Barzini (1965) states that some naive American criminals of Italian descent believe that criminal groups in their country belong to the Sicilian mafia: they "learned it by reading the newspapers" (p. 270, emphasis added). That criminal organization can reflect media influence is highlighted by Ianni (1974). He reports that Bro Squires (a pseudonym for), a prominent black narcotics operator in Newark, decided upon a paramilitary type of organization: "He got the idea from the movie the Battle for Algiers." Ianni states that the Bro Squires' organization was patterned after the movie: "And it worked" (p. 95). Vito recalls that he never heard the term Cosa Nostra used until after the revelations of Joseph

119

Valachi; then "low-level people," apparently influenced by Valachi, began to use it.*

ISSUE ONE: THE STRUCTURE OF ORGANIZED CRIME

Organized crime, as described by Vito, is a network of patrons having domination over a particular geographic area or perhaps an industry (for example, a garment center in New York). The patron is what Cressey (1969) refers to as the caporegime or boss. A boss is merely a "patron's patron." A patron will have available a network of informants and connections, partito (for example, with the police and other public officials, legitimate business-men, etcetera), as well as specialized operators (for example, enforcers, papermen, and money-movers). He will act as a center for information, a clearinghouse for criminal activities, assisting criminals to link up for specialized operations. He will serve as a "license commissioner," authorizing criminal, and sometimes legitimate, activities within his sphere of influence. Criminal activities in his territory not under his patronage (license) are outlaw operations, and the participants act without his "grace." If they are arrested, he will not intervene; if their activities conflict with those under his patronage, police raids or violence will result. Professional criminals who are not necessarily members of organized crime will often pay tribute to a patron, indicating rispetto, a word that literally means "respect" but that inclines toward approval and protection. This tribute enables the criminal to secure vital information and sometimes material aid – for example, firearms or stolen cars. Above all, it ensures that other criminals will not interfere with or jeopardize his operations.

---

*D. Smith (1976) argues that "it is no longer possible to say with certainty that there is or is not an organization called the Mafia. Accepted conclusions of labeling theory argue strongly that after a quarter century of having been labeled as mafiosi, a sense of group identification and accep-tance of the label would have occurred to a number of Italian-Americans even if there had been no basis for it previously. The characteristics of illicit marketplaces argue strongly that an entrepreneur labeled as a mafioso would have little incentive to deny it (except in certain law-enforcement circumstances), given the increased status and power that expectations associated with the label would carry" (p. 86). The latter point receives support in Vito's narrative and provides an example of W.I. Thomas' classic observation (1951): "If men define situations as real, they are real in their consequences" (p. 81).

INTERPRETATION AND IMPLICATIONS

There are examples of the exercise of patron domination in New York City. Several years ago, in a neighborhood noted for the extent of its patron control, criminals burglarized a famous restaurant (Ferrara's), which has no known connections with organized crime. However, the burglary was not "authorized" and thus indicated a lack of rispetto – the burglars were executed. In this same neighborhood, members of the Congress of Racial Equality (CORE) began picketing police headquarters when Italian-American boys gathered to taunt and throw rocks at them – the beginning of an ugly and difficult situation for the police. The patron (Genovese family) sent one of his men who Cressey (1969) reports "made a two-word, heart-warming appeal to the neighborhood boys' sense of social justice: 'Go home.' The boys went home" (p. 189). In another county, the lack of rispetto was aggravated by sacrilege: someone stole a gem-laden crown from a church. Joseph Profaci, the outraged patron, an ardent churchgoer, ordered the crown returned (which it was), and the sinner executed (which he was – strangled to death with a rosary).

If operating in an area without the express consent of the patron is dangerous, what about robbing those under his patronage? Vincent ("The Cat") Siciliano, the son of a murdered organized crime figure, did just that and was "summoned" (Siciliano, 1970).

> When we got to the cafe and those big shots started laying down the law and telling us that we knocked over one of their games, butter wouldn't melt in my mouth. I told them I was careful to ask if the game had any connections, and the other guys agreed and we all agreed that nobody had any idea in the whole world that the game had any connections.
>
> The way we always put it (the way you still put it) is that we didn't know they were "with anybody," or we didn't know they were "good people," which is like saying the guy is an American or an official something. Part of some organization. Not an outlaw.
>
> First they made us return the money. . . . Then they called us dumb, wild kids for not being careful and they started asking us where we got the tip on the game. (P. 55)

Vincent Teresa, an organized crime figure from New England, discusses partito and rispetto when he reports on his encounter with Joe Paterno – an encounter that almost cost him his life. Bernie has swindled Teresa out of $10,000, and Teresa went to Bernie's house, beat him up, and took back his money, and then some. It turns out that Joe Paterno is Bernie's patron. Paterno contacts Raymond Patriarca, New England crime boss and Teresa's patron, and demands that Teresa be killed. Teresa (1973) reports that

> Bernie had lied to Paterno. He said that I'd been told he was with Paterno before I slugged him, which was a lie, and he said I didn't

care who he was with, which was also a lie. If I had done those things, it would have meant that I had no respect for Paterno, that I was spitting in his face. Paterno had to put me in the bag. (However, when)he found out what really happened, they gave Bernie a terrible beating. (P. 108)

Organized crime provides the only semblance of government in a society of anarchy. Without the quasi-governmental function provided by organized crime patrons, the society of crime would be a Hobbesian nightmare. Reuter and Rubinstein (1978b) state that the mafia provides arbitration: "In an economy without conventional written contracts, there is obviously room for serious disagreements. These are hard to resolve" (p. 64).

Many bookmakers make payments to "wise guys" to ensure that when disputes arise they have effective representation. Sometimes these disputes are resolved on their merits. Sometimes they are resolved simply on the basis of the rank of the two arbitrators. It is critical to note that this arbitration is used only in a very restricted set of circumstances.

It is not used to collect from delinquent customers who are unable to meet their commitments as a result of either poor planning or over-indulgence. A legitimate bettor may be cut off and mildly harassed, but he will receive no threat from enforcers.* If, however, the dispute is with a "wise guy" or a "connected" person, then the arbitration system will be invoked. In particular, if it appears that there is deliberate intention by such persons to defraud the book-maker, then the Mafia man will be called in. This risk insurance is important to the bookmaker because people in the criminal trades are among the largest bettors, and are the customers most likely to flout him. (P. 64)

Throughout Vito's narrative, we are exposed to the operations of a network centered around Joe Paterno who, in turn, is part of a larger network with Carlo Gambino as patron at its center. We hear of other patron-centered networks, one with John Serratelli and Ralph Saludo, with Jerry Catena as patron, who is himself part of a larger network with Vito

---

*This would not be the case with a "connected" bookmaker. He would have available a network that includes enforcers (in some instances the bookmaker himself may also be an enforcer), and he would use them if he believed it worth the effort; if the expenditure of resources (violence) is deemed cost-effective. We have also seen in Vito's narrative that violence may be used to ensure rispetto.

Genovese as patron at its center. The network of Joe Bonanno becomes entangled with that of Gambino — a Bonanno family member is loan sharking in Paterno's area. From both of these situations we learn of a certain respect for territoriality. We also learn, however, that this concept has its limitations. Paterno explains to Vito that had he known about the situation with John Serratelli and Ralph Saludo, he could have intervened. He reports that he knows Jerry Catena very well and that something could have been worked out. Now that it is a fait accompli, however, it is too late to do anything. The way in which the network can be utilized is vividly described by Vito, using a hypothetical, but realistic, possibility. He describes how Paterno could research a witness and by utilizing "Nth-order zones" reach out to that person to secure a change in testimony.

R. Anderson (1965) traces the evolution of mafia in western Sicily and reports a trend toward bureaucratization (as enumerated by Blau, 1956) that is, a hierarchy of authority, specialization, a system of (in the case of mafia, unwritten) rules, and impartiality. He points to a similar trend in the United States as mafia became Cosa Nostra, although his American sources are questionable — for example, Joseph Valachi or the Saturday Evening Post. If we use Blau's (1956) criteria, organized crime as described by Vito does take on bureaucratic aspects — for example, it has a hierarchy (p. 19). However, Mouzelis (1968) points out that

> what makes an administration more or less bureaucratic from the hierarchical point of view is not the number of levels of authority, or the size of the span of control; the decisive criteria is whether or not the authority relations have a precise and impersonal character, as a result of the elaboration of rational rules. (P. 40)

The data do not indicate authority relations that are precise and impersonal, based on the "elaboration of rational rules." As noted in chapter 1, the history of Italian-American organized crime is more Byzantine than rational.

Organized crime as described by Vito also has a system of (unwritten but) explicit rules governing behavior. Mouzelis points out, however, that

> what makes an organization more or less bureaucratic is not simply the existence of rules, but the quality of these rules. Feudal administration also controlled organisational action through rules. But, the decisive difference between it and a bureaucracy is that these rules were not based on technical knowledge and rational thinking but on tradition. (P. 39)

Impartiality is missing. Only those of Italian heritage can qualify for membership. Vito reports that Joe Paterno achieved his position, at least in part, as a result of the influence and prestige of his father, don Antonio.

Nick Paterno, we are told, received a lucrative "no-show" job through the efforts of his brother.* We do not get a sense of bureaucracy in Vito's narrative. When Carlo Gambino meets Joe Bonanno on behalf of his client Joe Paterno, it could very well have been as two gang chieftains (modern versions of the feudal lord) seeking to avoid violence over territorial prerogatives – as opposed to a meeting between two leaders of an elaborate corporate entity. This seemingly minor problem required a top-level meeting. In bureaucratic organization procurators, persons empowered to negotiate, would have been sent to resolve the issue. Apparently there was also a need for <u>nuncio</u>, ceremonious representation of the principals, at this meeting. Only the boss himself could fulfill both roles (procurator and <u>nuncio</u>).

Joe Paterno's operations appear quite loose and, at times, almost accidental – his association with Vito is accidental. His accounting system is quite lax. He requires Vito to pay him 10 percent of his illegal earnings, but Vito fails to do this and Paterno either does not know or care. Paterno has apparently given out sums of money to trusted soldiers for loan sharking purposes but seems to have no real system of controls.†One has to wonder, for example, what would have happened to Paterno's money if "Kathy the Jew" had lost or otherwise disposed of her husband's book containing loan sharking records? There is the obvious danger involved in keeping detailed written records that makes bureaucracy in organized crime untenable.

Bureaucratic control is further complicated: important communications must be face-to-face, for security reasons. Vito explains that since there is fear of being overheard by bugs or taps, conversations are cryptic and often in a Sicilian dialect. (There are many dialects in Sicily, and Sicilians from different towns cannot easily understand each other's dialect.) This raises important questions about information on organized crime based on electronic surveillance – legal and illegal. Vito reports that although he was present and could hear the conversations clearly, he often did not know what

---

*Of course, Henry Ford II and David Rockefeller did not get their positions through <u>the New York Times</u>.

†Collins (1975) points out that "control" is a problem peculiar to patrimonial organizations. Bureaucracies develop, he argues, to overcome such problems: "patrimonial organizations cannot be very well controlled much beyond the immediate sight of a master" (p. 293). He notes that "when the geographic range becomes great enough, the organization collapses into feudalism."

Paterno and Gambino were talking about.* We must consider how much of the information secured through electronic surveillance is correctly "translated." It is, after all, these translated transcriptions that are made available to (some) researchers or to the general public in the case of the "De Cavalcante Tapes."†

While we do not get much in the way of a bureaucratic entity, we see some of the outward signs of a patrimonial organization. We are told that there is little or no trust of non-Italians and that Joe Paterno is closest (in business) with his own kin, his father and brother. Joe Paterno always refers to Vito by his Italian name, "Vitone," and when family bosses meet, there is kissing and embracing.

Organized crime is a practical accomplishment, and "doing organized crime" obviously requires skill and knowledge. However, unlike the professional thief, Paterno does not have "a complex of abilities and skills, just as do physicians, lawyers, or bricklayers," (Sutherland, 1972, p. 197). While the professional thief, according to Sutherland, has status based largely on his technical skills (p. 200),††one is left with the impression that the ability to command private violence is the item that makes Paterno an effective patron. To this must be added the time that he has to devote to maintaining his network (partito), an important variable for the effective patron. While he takes elaborate steps to avoid eavesdropping, Paterno keeps stolen checks in his house. He also participates directly in loan sharking, making overt threats to persons he has never met before, including one who is a lawyer. Vito points out that Paterno turns to Gambino for rather trivial

---

*Giddens (1976) states that "language involves the use of 'interpretive schemes' to make sense not only of what others say, but of what they mean: the constitution of 'sense' as an intersubjective accomplishment of mutual understanding in an ongoing exchange; and the use of contextual cues, as properties of the setting, as an integral part of the constitution and comprehension of meaning" (p. 104).

†With regard to these tapes, D. Smith (1980a) writes: "But what had been heard, and how had it been interpreted?" (p. 368). He argues that it was not studied in detail but involved a skimming "for clues to conversations that should be studied with greater care." But, what were the criteria for such skimming – prior expectations of what would be important?

††Chambliss' (1972) "Box-Man" (safecracker) disputes this claim: "This guy (Sutherland) makes a big issue out of a booster; kids shoplift and so do old broken-down housewives and these guys that eat dope and yellowjackets all the time. The shoplifters, there's nothing high classed about a shoplifter. Hell, they're the lowest there is" (p. 80). "Nobody has much to do with them" (p. 81).

matters. His own ineffectiveness has already cost him seven years of imprisonment. Despite apparent shortcomings, Paterno has been able to generate considerable income. According to a federal official with whom I spoke in March of 1980, Joe Paterno is living quite comfortably in Miami, Florida.*

R. Anderson (1965) argues that "in America, the traditional Mafia has evolved into a relatively complex organization which perpetuates selected features of the older peasant organization, but subordinates them to the requirements of a bureaucracy" (p. 310). The organization described by Vito, however, is not complex, nor does it add up to an entity that can comfortably be referred to as bureaucratic. Rather, it appears closer to the feudal structure that Hess (1973) and Blok (1974) attribute to the Sicilian mafia. Indeed, the amorphous quality makes organized crime difficult for government to deal with. The successful prosecution of a few leaders ("headhunting") does not have a significant impact on the organization; clients will shift to other patrons and continue their operations.†

ISSUE TWO: MEMBERSHIP, ROLES, AND RULES IN ORGANIZED CRIME

A. Anderson (1979) refers to four associate categories in the family she studied, but Vito does not seem to fit clearly into any of the associate categories. Vito describes himself as a "free-lance franchisee," a category that the literature on organized crime does not mention. Vito states that he believes he was being groomed for membership in the Gambino family,

---

*In 1978 Joe Paterno returned to Newark where on October 30 he was served with a subpoena ordering him to appear before the New Jersey State Commission of Investigation. Paterno appeared and citing his rights under the Fifth Amendment refused to answer any questions. He was subsequently granted immunity from prosecution by a superior court judge and ordered to testify. Should he return to New Jersey and fail to testify, Paterno could be imprisoned for contempt of court.

In 1978, Nicholas Paterno, then 56 years old, was sentenced to two and a half years by a federal court judge for his part in transporting stolen treasury checks and stocks across state lines.

†A historical analogy is provided by the sixteenth-seventeenth century struggle between the Spanish conquistadors and the Tairona of northern Colombia. While the Spanish easily conquered the highly centralized Inca and Aztec empires, the independent hierarchical organization of the hundreds of Tairona cities enabled them to successfully resist for more than 100 years. Unlike the Incas and Aztecs, there was no leader whose demise would throw the society into chaos (Hogue, 1980, p. 89).

which is his explanation for frequently being with Joe Paterno when the latter met with Carlo Gambino.

Vito provides some of the benefits of membership as opposed to associate status. The member, he states, is a genuine "insider." He can become involved in activities that nonmembers cannot or will not even be given the opportunity to become involved in. There is also Cressey's (1969) "sense of belonging," which Vito expresses as the macho aspect of organized crime — being one of the boys, commanding rispetto. Vito expresses delight in being able to shut down Neuman, a large corporation from which he has systematically embezzled money. Spergel (1964), in his study of "Racket-ville," noted that the racketeer had a great deal of status in his community; he exercised power over the criminal and conventional structure of the area. His relatives are also accorded high status and respect (pp. 18-19). Vito experiences this when he is first exposed to Joe Paterno at a christening celebration. He reports: "At the time I didn't know who Joseph Paterno was, although I noted that he seemed to be treated well, being catered to and shown a great deal of respect." In Mason, Vito is called upon to use his mafia influence to arrange for continued back-yard refuse collection. His neighbors do not seem to mind, indeed, apparently enjoy, having a mafioso in the neighborhood, and, as noted previously, Vito enjoyed the role.

Vito also notes an important (for him) disadvantage of being a member as opposed to being an associate: "If you are a member of the organization, you could be asked to do something that you did not want to do" — use violence, for example.

Roles

Cressey (1969) mentions several functional roles: enforcer, executioner, corrupter, and money-mover. He makes no mention of Vito's role, paperman. In Vito's narrative we experience two relatively fixed roles: enforcer and money-mover. Vito does not find any difference between enforcer and executioner, as does Cressey. Vito points out that persons involved in organized crime refer to inviduals who fill these roles by their specialty. That is, they are referred to as "our paperman" or money-mover. Vito is introduced as a paperman without any accompanying explanation, so we can presume a relatively fixed role. The same can be said for the position of money-mover — Meyer Lansky is described by Joe Paterno as a money-mover without any accompanying explanation. The terms enforcer, executioner, and corrupter are so descriptive that this type of assessment would be impossible. The data do not provide information on the latter role, although we hear that Paterno could reach into the prosecutor's office.

Rules

Giddens (1976) states that "a grasp of the resources used by members of society to generate social interaction is a condition of the social scientist's understanding of their conduct in just the same way it is for those members themselves" (p. 16). Vito, like the social scientist, has to learn what for others in organized crime is taken-for-granted mutual knowledge. Schutz (1971) points out that the "stranger to a culture can frequently discern items with greater clarity than members themselves who rely on the continuance of their customary way of life" (p. 104). Vito is observed learning the rules for "doing organized crime"; these are the rules for a skilled performance by any competent member (or would-be member) of organized crime. Through Vito the rules are made available for examination:

1. Always show rispetto to those who can command it.
2. Report any failure to show proper rispetto to one's patron immediately.
3. Violence must be used, even if only of a limited type, to ensure rispetto.
4. Only those with an Italian heritage can be fully accepted – can be stand-up persons.
5. Never ask for surnames.
6. Never mention the name of the family boss; if you need to use a name, mention your patron (caporegime).
7. Never ask questions about matters that do not directly concern you.
8. There are specific rules governing etiquette, concerning dress and speech when in the presence of the family boss – for example, do not make any comments unless the boss addresses you and address a boss as "don," as in don Carlo or don Giuseppe.
9. When present with bosses when they are discussing important business that is not your concern, avoid giving the impression that you are interested in what is being discussed.
10. A member of the organization must obey an order even when it is personally obnoxious to him – for example, using physical violence against a total stranger (or even a friend).
11. You cannot resort to violence in a dispute with a member of another family; instead you must go to your patron for assistance.
12. Do not use the telephone except to arrange for a meeting place, preferably in code, from which you will then travel to a safe place to discuss business.
13. Avoid mentioning specifics when discussing business – for example, names, dates, and places – beyond those absolutely necessary for understanding.
14. Keep your mouth shut – anything you hear, anything you see, stays with you, in your head; do not talk about it.

15. Do not ask unnecessary questions; the amount of information given to you is all you need to know to carry out instructions.

16. Share a percentage (10 percent?) of the proceeds of your illegal activities with your patron.

17. If your patron arranges for two parties to work together, he assumes responsibility for arbitrating any disputes between the parties.

ISSUE THREE: THE BUSINESS OF ORGANIZED CRIME

In Vito's narrative we are exposed to a wide variety of activities that are the business of organized crime. Vito, an ostensibly legitimate businessman, sought out Joe Paterno as his partner in the refuse business. Like other businessmen, Vito is interested in shortcuts; in this case, the power that Paterno, as organized crime, had available. Businesses that generate cut-throat competition are susceptible to what Clark and Hollinger (1977) refer to as normative incongruity: "For certain occupational behaviors we can identify conflicting interpretation as to whether a given act is an example of deviance or conformity" (p. 146). Societal norms may conflict with the norms of a particular business: "There are times when the normative expectations of the work organization are inconsistent with society's laws" (p. 143). Business groups can provide a set of rules for members that are more salient than legal codes and may encourage direct violations of law (p. 145). The presence of normative incongruity is an attraction for organized crime that can provide the enforcement necessary to ensure conformity to norms that violate the law. In the first chapter I noted the "services" rendered by Lepke and Gurrah in the fur industry in New York. The refuse business is one that traditionally been susceptible to organized crime influence.*

---

*In an effort to secure evidence of organized crime activity in the refuse industry in the Bronx, the FBI went into the garbage carting business. Several agents, using some old army sanitation trucks, opened American Automated Refuse in 1976. While they were able to secure a number of accounts, the service that they provided was so poor that they soon ran into trouble with the New York City Consumer Protection Agency – but not organized crime. In response, the FBI purchased four well-conditioned trucks and began to make a profit. They also succeeded in convicting Joseph Gambino, Carlo's cousin and a ranking member of his family. He had entered the United States illegally in 1957 and has been under a deportation order since 1967. Joseph Gambino received a 40-year sentence for his attempt to extort money from American Automated Refuse – a fee for being allowed to operate in the Bronx. The extortion attempt involved the beating of an FBI agent, which was videotaped.

Vito shows us that it is not necessary for organized crime to provide this service. When John Serratelli temporarily moves out of the "3 percent business," another person, an otherwise legitimate businessman, Jim Petro, moves in to take his place. Vito is able to do the same with small independent refuse collectors without any help from organized crime. However, neither can withstand the "entreaties" from organized crime. As essentially legitimate businessmen in a marginal or illegitimate enterprise, they cannot easily avail themselves of those agencies that are supposed to provide protection, for example, law enforcement. Access to private violence is a resource of organized crime, and illegitimate entrepreneurs who do not command private violence can be preyed upon by those who do. Schelling (1971) has argued that it is extortion, which is obviously dependent on the use of private violence or corrupt police, often both, that is <u>the</u> business of organized crime. Most illegal entrepreneurs, Schelling states, do not need organized crime. While they might find it useful, organized crime is simply not essential (pp. 646-47). Certainly this was true in the cases of Jim Petro and Vito Palermo. The availability of private violence, disciplined and efficient, is what makes organized crime a viable entity. While not sufficient in and of itself, violence as a resource is indispensable; it enables the quasi-government that is organized crime – a government without police has no existence. Thus, while there are no written licenses to practice organized crime, there are informal, but very real, equivalents, and there are real sanctions for "practicing without a license."

Organized crime involvement in legitimate business is indeed a reality. However, its importance has been exaggerated out of proportion by isolating organized crime from "white-collar" crime in general: "The semantic confusion is emphasized because 'organized crime in business is usually referred to as white collar crime, except when committed by racketeers who enter into business, in which case it is called organized crime, even though the criminal acts may be identical'" (Yeager, 1973, p. 65). When corporations, in violation of antitrust statutes, fix prices or otherwise agree to avoid or reduce competition, we have white-collar crime (Sutherland, 1949). When a group of refuse firms, under the guiding hands of a man whose name ends in a vowel, assigns territories and refrains from underbidding contracts for hauling garbage, we have organized crime.*

---

*D. Smith (1980a), in an effort to avoid this artificial division, proposes a "spectrum-based theory of enterprise," which starts from three basic assumptions: "that enterprise takes place across a spectrum that includes both business and certain kinds of crime; that behavioral theory regarding organizations in general and business in particular can be applied to the entire spectrum; and that, while theories about conspiracy and ethnicity have some pertinance to organized crime, they are clearly subordinate to a theory of enterprise" (p. 370). The "Great Electrical Equipment Conspiracy,"

Through Vito's discussion of Joe Paterno, we see how an organized crime patron can act as a catalyst for conventional crime.* Vito points out that his checks-and-securities operation required the services of a person who had extensive contacts with all types of criminals. Paterno acts as a clearinghouse, linking up specialized operators (for example, burglars with a paperman) and providing money, information, and connections, thus encouraging all types of crime, including robbery. During at least one of these "sponsored" robberies, a guard was killed. There appears to be no restriction on the type of activity that can be engaged in by members of organized crime (except drug trafficking, which was a prohibited activity for a time). While organized crime can be a rather haphazard operation, it is clearly a threat to legitimate persons who become victims of labor and business racketeering, loan sharking, and sponsored robberies and burglaries. A. Anderson (1979) states that her research shows that the crime family she studied, while not necessarily representative of others, "is neither of major significance in the economy of the city (she does not reveal the city)where it operates not a serious threat to its legitimate business competitors or the customers of its illegal enterprises" (p. 140). Joe Paterno, however, is clearly a threat to customers of his legitimate and illegitimate businesses, as the incidents involving Walter Kiddie, Neuman, Berg and the Schuman brothers indicate. Paterno helped to compromise the integrity of banks and banking officials and encouraged the theft of stocks and bonds by providing an outlet for their disposal.

Just as Ianni (1972) found that the Lupollos were moving quite extensively into legitimate enterprises, we find Paterno doing the same. He enters the refuse business with Vito, and we learn that he is also connected with the disposal end of this business. In addition, Paterno owns a home-improvement firm, All-State Construction Company, and is heavily into real estate with holdings apparently worth in the seven figures.

---

for example, involved executives of corporations such as General Electric and Westinghouse in a bid-rigging conspiracy similar to that of Vito and John Serratelli (see R. Smith, 1961a, 1961b). Clinard et al. (1979) find the term white-collar crime too broad. They call crime committed for the benefit of the corporation "corporate crime," as opposed to acts that victimize the corporation, for example, embezzlement, which they refer to as "occupational crime" (p. 18). See also Ross (1980).

*Jackson (1969) argues that "organized criminals avoid safes and checks not because they find such activities loathsome, but because there is no way to insure even a modicum of safety and monopoly" (p. 30).

SOME POLICY IMPLICATIONS OF THE DATA

What does Vito's narrative offer with respect to responding to organized crime? There are two basic strategies in common use: increasing the risks of doing business and reducing the opportunity for profit. The first strategy entails stiff penalities for, and intensive investigation of, organized criminal activities. Vito tells us, however, that increased penalties for usury caused Joe Paterno to change his operation – not give up loan sharking. Paterno merely avoided direct involvement, passing the risk, along with some of the profit, to others under his control The second strategy involves attempts to break the monopoly over certain goods and services enjoyed by illegal entrepreneurs. This has been most noticeable in gambling.

The legalization of lotteries, off-track betting, and casino gambling by several states, however, has been based on financial considerations and only secondarily on its usefulness as a means of reducing profit opportunities for organized crime (if this was ever seriously considered at all). As a result, the legalization of gambling in the United States may be accompanied by an increase in the number of people who gamble. In the United States, under the Nevada model,* gambling is actively promoted by, or with the approval of, government. Reducing profit opportunities in gambling carries additional risks. As noted in the data, the business of organized crime is quite dynamic. If gambling profit is reduced, we can expect displacement into other areas of opportunity. In the "De Cavalcante Tapes" it was revealed that when other sources of income were not readily available, the <u>amici</u> took to burglary, robbery, and drug trafficking (which was a prohibited activity at the time). The Campisis went on their robbery and murder rampage as a direct result of decreasing profits from gambling. Vito notes that don Antonio made a great deal of money during the war in the black market. If gas rationing is imposed, this will create new opportunity for organized crime.†

Organized crime evolved out of moralistic laws that created opportunity for certain innovative actors. As circumstances changed, so did available opportunity, and organized crime proved quite dynamic. From essentially "goods and services" to racketeering and legitimate business, organized

---

*Nevada reportedly leads the nation in personal bankruptcies, suicides, and deaths from cirrhosis of the liver (Satchell, 1979, p. 9). An alternative model is offered in England where gambling is tolerated, not in an effort to generate revenue but because the alternative appears even more socially harmful (Skolnick, 1978, pp. 337-39).

†The FBI reports that during the 1973 gas crisis they experienced the hijacking of gas trucks for the first time. Recent news reports indicate an increase in such hijackings.

crime has managed to adapt to changing laws and social and economic conditions. When interest in the stocks and bonds market mushroomed in the 1960s, organized crime found new opportunity. When certain commodities are scarce, the black market is created. When expansion of illegitimate business is no longer possible or profitable, conventional crime, real estate speculation, and other legitimate outlets are utilized for profit.*

---

*The New York Times (November 30, 1980: E5; Brown, 1980) reports that New Jersey is experiencing a takeover of the toxic-waste disposal business by organized crime members from the refuse industry.

References

Abadinsky, Howard. 1981. Organized Crime. Boston: Allyn and Bacon.

Albini, Joseph L. 1971. The American Mafia: Genesis of a Legend. New York: Appleton-Century-Crofts.

Anderson, Annelise Graebner. 1979. The Business of Organized Crime. Stanford, Calif.: Hoover Institution Press.

Anderson, Robert T. 1965. "From Mafia to Cosa Nostra." American Journal of Sociology 71 (November): 302-10.

Aronson, Harvey. 1978. Deal. New York: Ballantine Books.

Asbury, Herbert. 1928. Gangs of New York. New York: Alfred A. Knopf.

Bacherach, Samuel B., and Edward J. Lawler. 1976. "The Perception of Power." Social Forces 55 (September): 123-34.

Ball, Donald W. 1970. "The Problematics of Respectability." In Deviance and Respectability, edited by Jack D. Douglas. New York: Basic Books.

Barzini, Luigi. 1977. "Italians in New York: The Way We Were in 1929." New York Magazine, April 4. 1977, pp. 33-38.

_____. 1965. The Italians. New York: Atheneum.

Becker, Howard S. 1973. Outsiders: Studies in the Sociology of Deviance. New York: Free Press.

REFERENCES

Bell, Daniel. 1964. The End of Ideology. Glencoe, Ill.: Free Press.

Bequai, August. 1979. Organized Crime: The Fifth Estate. Lexington, Mass.: D.C. Heath.

Berger, Meyer. 1944. "Lepke's Reign of Crime Lasted Over 12 Murder-Strewn Years." New York Times, March 5, 1944, p. 30.

Blau, Peter M. 1956. Bureaucracy in Modern Society. New York: Random House.

Block, Alan A. 1978. "History and the Study of Organized Crime." Urban Life 6 (January): 455-74.

_____. 1975. "Lepke, Kid Twist and the Combination: Organized Crime in New York City, 1930-1944." Ph.D. dissertation, University of California-Los Angeles.

Blok, Anton. 1974. The Mafia of a Sicilian Village, 1860-1960: A Study of Violent Peasant Entrepreneurs. London: William Cowes Sons.

Boissevain, Jeremy. 1974. Friends of Friends: Networks, Manipulators and Coalitions. Oxford, England: Basil Blackwell.

Brenner, Marie. 1981. "The Godfather's Child," New York Magazine (March 2): 18-20.

Brill, Steven. 1978. The Teamsters. New York: Simon and Schuster.

Brown, Michael H. 1980. "New Jersey Cleans Up Its Pollution Act." New York Times Magazine, November 23, 1980, pp. 142-46.

Capeci, Jerry. 1978. "Tieri: The Most Powerful Mafia Chieftain." New York Magazine, August 21, 1978, pp. 22-26.

Chambliss, William. 1975. "On the Paucity of Original Research on Organized Crime: A Footnote to Galliher and Cain." American Sociologist 10 (August): 36-39.

_____. 1972. Box-Man: A Professional Thief's Journey. New York: Harper & Row.

Chandler, David Leon. 1975. Brothers in Blood: The Rise of the Criminal Brotherhoods. New York: E. P. Dutton.

Clark, John P., and Richard Hollinger. 1977. "On the Feasibility of Empirical Studies of White-Collar Crime." In Theory in Criminology: Contemporary Views, edited by Robert F. Meier. Beverly Hills, Calif.: Sage.

Clinard, Marshall B., Peter C. Yeager, Jeanne Brissette, David Petrashek, and Elizabeth Harries. 1979. Illegal Corporate Behavior. Washington, D.C.: U.S. Government Printing Office.

Collins, Randall. 1975. Conflict Sociology. New York: Academic Press.

Connable, Alfred, and Edward Silberfarb. 1967. Tigers of Tammany: Nine Men Who Ran New York. New York: Holt, Rinehart and Winston.

Cook, Fred J. 1972. "Purge of the Greasers." In Mafia, U.S.A., edited by Nicholas Gage. New York: Dell.

Cornelisen, Ann. 1980. Strangers and Pilgrims: The Last Italian Migration. New York: Holt, Rinehart and Winston.

Cressey, Donald R. 1972. Criminal Organization: Its Elementary Forms. New York: Harper & Row.

_____. 1969. Theft of the Nation. New York: Harper & Row.

_____. 1967a. "The Functions and Structure of Criminal Syndicates." In Task Force Report: Organized Crime, edited by Task Force on Organized Crime. Washington, D.C.: U.S. Government Printing Office.

_____. 1967b. "Methodological Problems in the Study of Organized Crime as a Social Problem." Annals 374 (November): 101-12.

De Franco, Edward J. 1973. Anatomy of a Scam: A Case Study of a Planned Bankruptcy by Organized Crime. Washington, D.C.: U.S. Government Printing Office.

Diapoulas, Peter, and Steven Linakis. 1976. The Sixth Family. New York: E. P. Dutton.

Ditton, Jason. 1974. Part-Time Crime: An Ethnography of Fiddling and Pilferage. London: Macmillan.

Durkheim, Emile. 1951. Suicide. New York: Free Press.

Edelman, Bernard. 1980. "Eight Years Under Cover." Police Magazine, July 1980, pp. 45-49.

REFERENCES

Englemann, Larry. 1979. Intemperance: The Lost War against Liquor. New York: Free Press.

Feiden, Doug. 1979. "The Great Getaway: The Inside Story of the Lufthansa Robbery." New York Magazine, June 4, 1979, pp. 37-42.

Fisher, Sethard. 1975. "Review of the Black Mafia." Contemporary Sociology 4 (May): 83-84.

Fitzgerald, F. Scott. 1925. The Great Gatsby. New York: Charles Scribner's Sons.

Franks, Lucinda. 1977. "An Obscure Gangster Is Emerging as the New Mafia Chief in New York." New York Times, March 17, 1977, pp. 1, 34.

Fried, Albert. 1980. The Rise and Fall of the Jewish Gangster in America. New York: Holt, Rinehart and Winston.

Gage, Nicholas. 1974. "Questions Are Raised on Lucky Luciano Book." New York Times, December 17, 1974, pp. 1, 28.

Galliher, John F., and James A. Cain. 1974. "Citation Support for the Mafia Myth in Criminology Textbooks." American Sociologist 9 (May): 68-74.

Gambino, Richard. 1974. Blood of My Blood: The Dilemma of the Italian-Americans. Garden City, N.Y.: Doubleday.

"Gang Kills Suspect in Alien Smuggling." 1931. New York Times, September 11, 1931, p. 1.

"Gang Linked to Union Charged at Trial." 1934. New York Times, January 31, 1934, p. 8.

Gasper, Louis C. 1969. "Organized Crime: An Economic Analysis." Ph.D. dissertation, Duke University.

Giddens, Anthony. 1976. New Rules of Sociological Method: A Postive Critique of Interpretative Sociologies. New York: Basic Books.

Goffman, Erving. 1974. Frame Analysis: An Essay on the Organization of Experience. New York: Harper & Row.

_____. 1973. The Presentation of Self in Everyday Life. Woodstock, N.Y.: Overlook Press.

Gosch, Martin A., and Richard Hammer. 1974. The Last Testment of Lucky Luciano. Boston: Little, Brown.

Hess, Henner. 1973. Mafia and Mafioso: The Structure of Power. Lexington, Mass.: D.C. Heath.

Hibbert, Christopher. 1966. Garibaldi and His Enemies. Boston: Little, Brown.

Hobsbawn, Eric. 1959. Social Bandits and Primitive Rebels. Glencoe, Ill.: Free Press.

Hogue, Warren. 1980. "First Look at a Lost City." New York Times Magazine, November 30, 1980, pp. 42-44, 80, 82, 89-96.

Homans, George C. 1974. Social Behavior: Its Elementary Forms. New York: Harcourt Brace Jovanovich.

Homer, Frederic C. 1974. Guns and Garlic. West Lafayette, Ind.: Purdue University Press.

Ianni, Francis A. J. 1974. Black Mafia: Ethnic Succession in Organized Crime. New York: Simon and Schuster.

_____. 1972. A Family Business: Kinship and Social Control in Organized Crime. New York: Russell Sage Foundation.

Inciardi, James A. 1975. Careers in Crime. Chicago: Rand McNally.

Inciardi, James A., Alan A. Block, and Lyle A. Hallowell. 1977. Historical Approaches to Crime. Beverly Hills, Calif.: Sage.

"Informer Glad to Help F.B.I. Catch Mobster." 1980. New York Times. October 5, 1980, p. 61.

Jackson, Bruce. 1969. A Thief's Primer. London: Macmillan.

Katcher, Leo. 1959. The Big Bankroll: The Life and Times of Arnold Rothstein. New York: Harper and Brothers.

Kidner, John. 1976. Crimaldi: Contract Killer. Washington, D.C.: Acropolis Books.

Klockars, Carl B. 1974. The Professional Fence. New York: Free Press.

REFERENCES

Landesco, John. 1968. Organized Crime in Chicago. Chicago: University of Chicago Press.

Lasswell, Harold D., and Jerimiah B. McKenna. 1972. The Impact of Organized Crime on an Inner-City Community. New York: Policy Sciences Center.

Logan, Andy. 1970. Against the Evidence: The Becker-Rosenthal Affair. New York: McCall.

Maas, Peter. 1968. The Valachi Papers. New York: G. P. Putnam's Sons.

McConaughy, John. 1931. From Cain to Capone: Racketeering Down the Ages. New York: Brentano's.

Mack, John A. 1973. "The 'Organized' and 'Professional' Labels Criticised." International Journal of Criminology and Penology 1 (May): 106-16.

Maltz, Michael D. 1975. "Policy Issues in Organized and White-Collar Crime." In Crime and Criminal Justice, edited by John D. Gardiner and Michael A. Mulkey. Lexington, Mass.: D. C. Heath.

Martin, Raymond. 1963. Revolt in the Mafia. New York, Duell, Sloane and Pearce.

Matza, David. 1969. Becoming Deviant. Englewood Cliffs, N.J.: Prentice-Hall.

Meskil, Paul. 1977. "Meet the New Godfather." New York Magazine, February 28, 1977, pp. 28-32.

_____. 1973. Don Carlo: Boss of Bosses. New York: Popular Library.

Messick, Hank. 1973. Lansky. New York: Berkley.

Mitchell, Greg. 1980. "Ordeal of a Prosecution Witness." New York Times Magazine, November 16, 1980, pp. 106-20.

Morris, Norval, and Gordon Hawkins. 1970. The Honest Politicians Guide to Crime Control. Chicago: University of Chicago Press.

Mouzelis, Nicos P. 1968. Organization and Bureaucracy: An Analysis of Modern Theories. Chicago: Aldine.

Nelli, Humbert S. 1976. The Business of Crime. New York: Oxford University Press.

"New Gang Methods Replace Those of Eastman's Days." 1923. New York Times, September 9, 1923, p. 3.

Packer, Herbert L. 1968. The Limits of the Criminal Sanction. Stanford, Calif.: Stanford University Press.

Pantaleone, Michele. 1966. The Mafia and Politics. New York: Coward and McCann.

Plate, Thomas, and the Editors of New York Magazine. 1972. The Mafia at War. New York: New York Magazine Press.

Post, Henry. 1981. "'The Warehouse Sting,'" New York Magazine (February 2): 31-34.

"Racket Chief Slain by Gangster Gunfire." 1931. New York Times, April 16, 1931, p. 1.

Reuter, Peter, and Jonathan Rubinstein. 1978a. Bookmaking in New York. New York: Policy Sciences Center. (A preliminary, unpublished draft.)

_____. 1978b. "Fact, Fancy, and Organized Crime." Public Interest 53 (Fall): 45-67.

_____. 1977. Numbers: The Routine Racket. New York: Policy Sciences Center. (A preliminary, unpublished draft.)

Rock, Paul. 1973. Making People Pay. London: Routledge and Kegan Paul.

Ross, Irwin. 1980. "How Lawless are the Big Companies?" Fortune, December 1, 1980, pp. 57-58, 62-64.

Salerno, Ralph, and John S. Tompkins. 1969. The Crime Confederation. Garden City, N.Y.: Doubleday.

Sann, Paul. 1971. Kill the Dutchman: The Story of Dutch Schultz. New York: Popular Library.

Satchell, Michael. 1979. "Atlantic City's Great Gold Rush." Parade, June 10, 1979, pp. 8-10.

Schelling, Thomas C. 1971. "What is the Business of Organized Crime?" American Scholar 40 (Autumn): 643-52.

"Schultz Product of the Dry Era." 1933. New York Times, January 22, 1933, p. 23.

REFERENCES

Schumacher, Edward. 1980. "Killing of Bruno Prompts Worry over Gang War." New York Times, March 23, 1980, p. 16.

Schutz, Alfred. 1971. Collected Papers II: Studies in Social Theory. The Hague: Martinus Nijhoff.

Seedman, Albert A. 1974. Chief! New York: Arthur Fields.

Seidman, Harold. 1938. Labor Czars: A History of Labor Racketeering. New York: Liveright.

Seigel, Max H. 1976. "2 Named in Theft from Union Fund." New York Times, July 27, 1976, p. 60.

Serao, Ernesto. 1911a. "The Truth about the Camorra." Outlook 98 (July 28); 717-26.

_____. 1911b. "The Truth about the Camorra: Part Two." Outlook 98 (August 5): 778-87.

Shaw, Clifford R. 1966. The Jack-Roller: A Delinquent Boy's Own Story. Chicago: University of Chicago Press.

Siciliano, Vincent. 1970. Unless They Kill Me First. New York: Hawthorn Books.

Simmel, Georg. 1950. The Sociology of Georg Simmel. Translated and edited by Kurt Wolff. New York: Free Press.

Skolnick, Jerome H. 1978. House of Cards: Legalization and Control of Casino Gambling. Boston: Little, Brown.

Smith, Dwight C., Jr. 1980a. "Paragons, Pariahs, and Pirates: A Spectrum-Based Theory of Enterprise." Crime and Delinquency 26 (July): 358-86.

_____. 1980b. "Review of the Business of Organized Crime." Crime and Delinquency 26 (January): 99-100.

_____. 1976. "Mafia: The Prototypical Alien Conspiracy." Annals 423 (January): 75-88.

_____. 1975. The Mafia Mystique. New York: Basic Books.

Smith, Richard Austin. 1961a. "The Incredible Electrical Conspiracy." Fortune, May 1961, pp. 161-64, 210, 212, 217-18, 221-22, 224.

_____. 1961b. "The Incredible Electrical Conspiracy." Fortune, April 1961, pp. 132-37, 170, 175-76, 179-80.

Smith, Sherwin D. 1963. "35 Years Ago: Arnold Rothstein was Mysteriously Murdered and Left a Racket Empire Up for Grabs." New York Times Magazine, October 27, 1963, p. 96.

Spergel, Irving. 1964. Racketeville, Slumtown, Haulberg. Chicago: University of Chicago Press.

State of New Jersey v. Ruggerio Boiardo, et. al. 1979. Indictment Number SGJ49-78-7 (May 23).

Sullivan, Joseph F. 1980. "Jersey Man in Abscam Case Is Experienced with Inquiries." New York Times, March 9, 1980, p. 20.

_____. 1972. "Underworld Purchase of Land in Meadowlands Is Investigated." New York Times, August 9, 1972, p. 41.

Sutherland, Edwin H. 1972. The Professional Thief. Chicago. University of Chicago Press.

_____. 1949. White Collar Crime. New York: Holt, Rinehart and Winston.

Talese, Gay. 1971. Honor Thy Father. New York: World.

Task Force on Organized Crime. 1976. Organized Crime. Washington, D.C.: U.S. Government Printing Office.

_____. 1967. Task Force Report: Organized Crime. Washington, D.C.: U.S. Government Printing Office.

Teresa, Vincent, with Thomas C. Renner. 1973. My Life in the Mafia. Garden City, N.Y.: Doubleday.

Thomas, W. I. 1951. Social Behavior and Personality: Contributions of W. I. Thomas to Theory and Social Research. Edited by Edmund H. Volhart. New York: Social Science Research Council.

Thrasher, Frederic Milton. 1968. The Gang: A Study of 1,313 Gangs in Chicago. Chicago: University of Chicago Press. (An abridged edition of the 1927 original.)

Toby, Jackson. 1958. "Hoodlum or Business Man: An American Dilemma." In The Jews: Social Patterns of an American Group, edited by Marshall Sklare. Glencoe, Ill.: Free Press.

REFERENCES

Turkus, Burton, and Sid Feder. 1951. Murder, Inc.: The Story of the Syndicate. New York: Farrar, Straus and Young.

Tyler, Gus. 1975. "Review of the Black Mafia." Crime and Delinquency 21 (April): 178-79.

Tyler, Gus, ed. 1963. "Combating Organized Crime." Annals 347 (May).

Tyler, Gus, ed. 1962. Organized Crime in America. Ann Arbor: University of Michigan Press.

U.S. Drug Enforcement Administration, Office of Intelligence. 1980. Outlaw Motorcycle Gangs: An Interim Report. Washington, D.C.: mimeo.

Villano, Anthony. 1978. Brick Agent. New York: Ballantine Books.

Waggoner, Walter H. 1975. "10 to Be Queried About Organized Crime." New York Times, May 8, 1977, p. 84.

Walsh, Marilyn E. 1977. The Fence. Westport, Conn.: Greenwood Press.

Weber, Max. 1968. Economy and Society. Edited by Guenther Roth and Claus Wiltich. New York: Bedminister Press.

Whyte, William Foote. 1961. Street Corner Society. Chicago: University of Chicago Press.

Wolf, Eric R. 1966. "Kinship, Friendship, and Patron-Client Relations in Complex Societies." In Social Anthropology of Complex Societies, edited by Michael Banton. London: Tavistock.

Wolfe, Tom. 1970. Radical Chic and Mau-Mauing the Flak Catchers. New York: Farrar, Straus and Giroux.

Wrong, Dennis. 1970. Max Weber. Englewood Cliffs, N.J.: Prentice-Hall.

_____. 1968. "Some Problems in Defining Social Power." American Journal of Sociology 73 (May): 673-81.

Yeager, Matthew G. 1973. "The Gangster as White Collar Criminal: Organized Crime and Stolen Securities." Issues in Criminology 8 (Spring): 49-73.

Author Index

Abadinsky, Howard, 38
Albini, Joseph L., 37
Anderson, Annelise Graebner,
 21, 31, 35, 44, 126, 131
Anderson, Robert T., 123,
 126
Aronson, Harvey, 90n
Asbury, Herbert, 4

Bacherach, Samuel, 38
Ball, Donald W., 116
Barzini, Luigi, 13, 15, 17,
 18, 118, 119
Becker, Howard S., 48, 50,
 117
Bell, Daniel, 3, 9
Bequai, August, 39
Berger, Meyer, 6
Blau, Peter M., 123
Block, Alan A., 6, 40, 41
Blok, Anton, 15, 16, 126
Boissevain, Jeremy, 19, 20
Brenner, Marie, 94n
Brill, Steven, 53n
Brown, Michael H., 133n

Cain, James A., 40
Capeci, Jerry, 42
Chambliss, William, 46,
 125n

Chandler, David Leon, 14
Clark, John P., 129
Clinard, Marshall B., 131n
Collins, Randall, 18, 88,
 124n
Connable, Alfred, 4
Cook, Fred J., 41
Cornelisen, Ann, 19
Cressey, Donald R., 11, 12,
 21, 26, 27, 35, 41, 43,
 120, 121, 127

De Franco, Edward J., 30
Diapoulas, Peter, 10n
Ditton, Jason, 118
Durkheim, Emile, 117

Edelman, Bernard, 107n
Englemann, Larry, 4n

Feiden, Doug, 38
Fisher, Sethard, 46
Fitzgerald, F. Scott, 5
Franks, Lucinda, 42
Fried, Albert 6, 7

Gage, Nicholas, 40
Galliher, John F., 40
Gambino, Richard, 13, 16, 17,
 18

*The index was prepared with the assistance of Alisa Abadinsky.

AUTHOR INDEX

Toby, Jackson, 9
Tompkins, John S., 38
Turkus, Burton, 93n
Tyler, Gus, 3, 35, 46n

Villano, Anthony, 40

Waggoner, Walter H., 60n
Walsh, Marilyn E., 30
Weber, Max, 38
Whyte, William Foote, 46, 48
Wolf, Eric R., 20
Wolfe, Tom, 116n
Wrong, Dennis, 13, 38

Yeager, Matthew G., 130

Subject Index

SUBJECT INDEX

Valachi, Joseph, 8, 94, 95n, 121
Vario, Paul, 38, 107n
Volstead Act, 6

wire-tapping (see electronic
   surveillance)
Witness Protection Program, 49,
   67, 67n, 90n, 110-114
Workman, Charles ("Charlie the
   Bug"), 93n

Yale, Frank (Uale), 7

Zerrilli, Joseph, 18
Zwillman, Abner ("Longie"), 9

About the Author

HOWARD ABADINSKY, now an Assistant Professor of Criminal Justice at Western Carolina University, was a New York State Parole Officer for 14 years. He has authored several books on criminal justice including a textbook entitled <u>Organized Crime</u> (Allyn and Bacon, 1981).

Professor Abadinsky holds graduate degrees from Fordham University and New York University and received a certificate in "Investigating Organized Crime" from the North Carolina Justice Academy.